A faithful life is the sum of a million daily decis[...]
This is why *8 Habits for Growth* is so importan[...]
cally, and simply shares the secrets to life with Je[...]
that form our hearts and are used by the Spirit to sanctify us into spiritual maturity. Pastoral, wise, and practical, this will be a book every pastor will need to have at the ready to give to their people and a book every family should have in order to form habits for spiritual growth.

DANIEL DARLING, Senior VP, NRB, and bestselling author of several books

As one writer has said, beautiful people do not just happen. Becoming the best version of ourselves—whether it be professionally, relationally, personally, or otherwise—requires a commitment to practices that get us there. To flourish optimally as people of God, we also must habituate several soul-nourishing practices. For those who need a field guide for this pursuit, Darryl has written a fabulous field guide.

SCOTT SAULS, senior pastor, Christ Presbyterian Church, Nashville, TN

It's hard to imagine a more "user friendly" book for Christians who want to cultivate personal habits for spiritual growth! This book is especially ideal for small groups and discussion groups to work through together. Darryl Dash has given a wonderful gift to the church with this edifying, practical, and Christ-honoring book.

GAVIN ORTLUND, pastor of First Baptist Church, Ojai, and author of *Why God Makes Sense in a World That Doesn't*

8 Habits for Growth is like a conversation with a grounded, thoughtful, faithful friend who wants nothing more than to encourage you in your walk with Christ—a spiritual coach who buys you a coffee and a donut and shares with you some things that worked for them (and multitudes of others). The "clean-slate policy" of just picking yourself up and moving on if you flounder is especially grace-filled and refreshing. In Darryl's own words: "The habits are good, but the habits aren't the point. The point is that we were made to know and worship God." This book will help you get there.

KAREN STILLER, author of *The Minister's Wife*, coeditor of *Faith Today* magazine

This wise and inspiring book is packed with profound insights and practical applications! Highly accessible and immediately actionable, Darryl's powerful book can change the way you move through the world.

KEN SHIGEMATSU, pastor, Tenth Church, Vancouver, BC, and bestselling author of *God in My Everything*

Healthy habits are fundamental to our flourishing as Christians. But habits are hard, and developing new habits—or maintaining existing ones—is daunting. This is an accessible, practical, and actionable book—perfect for small groups, families, and friends seeking sustainable growth in a culture of fads and quick fixes.

BRETT MCCRACKEN, senior editor at The Gospel Coalition and author of *The Wisdom Pyramid: Feeding Your Soul in a Post-Truth World*

With welcoming clarity, *8 Habits for Growth* offers the reader a cup of encouragement and food for discernment in the holy care of body, mind, and spirit for the purpose-filled pilgrimage ahead. Fortunately, there is nothing we can do to earn grace. And fortunately, we have a model in Jesus of God's best for us. In light of these blessings, Darryl Dash provides a thoughtful and thorough guide on how to number our days

CAROLYN WEBER, professor of literature and award-winning author

You make decisions, but eventually your decisions make you. In his new book *8 Habits for Growth*, Darryl Dash does a wonderful job of cutting through the noise that has become life today to isolate eight critical habits that, practiced regularly, will benefit you for years to come. These habits will become investments that will pay off for the rest of your life.

CAREY NIEUWHOF, Founding Pastor, Connexus Church

In this immensely practical and hopeful volume, Darryl Dash reminds us that the Christian life is formed in us through the ordinary habits of our days. We often want spiritual transformation to be quick, but Dash points us to eight small habits—showing us how things like decluttering and caring for our bodies work alongside corporate worship, prayer, and Bible reading—to actually experience transformation. *8 Habits for Growth* is the resource individuals, parents, and church leaders need to help themselves and others experience real gospel fruit.

ASHLEY HALES, author, pastor's wife, and host of the *Finding Holy* podcast

8 HABITS FOR GROWTH

*A Simple Guide
to Becoming
More Like Christ*

DARRYL DASH

MOODY PUBLISHERS

CHICAGO

© 2021 by
DARRYL DASH

All rights reserved. No part of this book may be reproduced in any form without permission in writing from the publisher, except in the case of brief quotations embodied in critical articles or reviews.

Unless otherwise indicated, all Scripture quotations are from the ESV® Bible (The Holy Bible, English Standard Version®), copyright © 2001 by Crossway, a publishing ministry of Good News Publishers. Used by permission. All rights reserved.

Scripture quotations marked (NIV) are taken from the Holy Bible, New International Version®, NIV®. Copyright © 1973, 1978, 1984, 2011 by Biblica, Inc.™ Used by permission of Zondervan. All rights reserved worldwide. www.zondervan.com The "NIV" and "New International Version" are trademarks registered in the United States Patent and Trademark Office by Biblica, Inc.™

Scripture quotations marked CSB have been taken from the Christian Standard Bible®, Copyright © 2017 by Holman Bible Publishers. Used by permission. Christian Standard Bible® and CSB® are federally registered trademarks of Holman Bible Publishers.

Edited by Connor Sterchi
Interior design: Brandi Davis
Cover design: Erik M. Peterson
Author photo: Froz'n Motion Photography

Library of Congress Cataloging-in-Publication Data

Names: Dash, Darryl, author.
Title: 8 habits for growth : a simple guide to becoming more like Christ / Darryl Dash.
Other titles: Eight habits for growth
Description: Chicago, IL : Moody Publishers, [2021] | Includes bibliographical references. | Summary: "The key to life transformation-for yourself and then for others-is building habits that become part of your life. In 8 Habits for Growth, Darryl Dash wants to show you the eight long-term practices-all very doable-that will lead to permanent growth if you incorporate them into your life"-- Provided by publisher.
Identifiers: LCCN 2021014628 (print) | LCCN 2021014629 (ebook) | ISBN 9780802423658 | ISBN 9780802499745 (ebook)
Subjects: LCSH: Christian life. | Spiritual formation. | BISAC: RELIGION / Christian Living / Leadership & Mentoring | RELIGION / Christian Ministry / Discipleship
Classification: LCC BV4501.3 .D3737 2021 (print) | LCC BV4501.3 (ebook) | DDC 248.4--dc23
LC record available at https://lccn.loc.gov/2021014628
LC ebook record available at https://lccn.loc.gov/2021014629

Originally delivered by fleets of horse-drawn wagons, the affordable paperbacks from D. L. Moody's publishing house resourced the church and served everyday people. Now, after more than 125 years of publishing and ministry, Moody Publishers' mission remains the same—even if our delivery systems have changed a bit. For more information on other books (and resources) created from a biblical perspective, go to www.moodypublishers.com or write to:

Moody Publishers
820 N. LaSalle Boulevard
Chicago, IL 60610

1 3 5 7 9 10 8 6 4 2

Printed in the United States of America

With gratitude for Edward and Christina Crocker
and Denise Dash, who taught me about Jesus
through their words and their lives.

"I am reminded of your sincere faith, a faith that dwelt first
in your grandmother Lois and your mother Eunice and now,
I am sure, dwells in you as well." (2 Timothy 1:5)

CONTENTS

FOREWORD 9

INTRODUCTION 13

HABIT #1: Make Time 21

HABIT #2: Rest and Refresh 49

HABIT #3: Engage the Bible 79

HABIT #4: Speak with God 109

HABIT #5: Worship and Belong 135

HABIT #6: Care for Your Body 173

HABIT #7: Simplify and Prioritize 201

HABIT #8: Go the Distance 227

APPENDIX: Sample Practices 257

RECOMMENDED RESOURCES /
 ABOUT GOSPEL FOR LIFE 262

ACKNOWLEDGMENTS 263

NOTES 265

FOREWORD

AT SIXTEEN, I BECAME a follower of Jesus. Having spent most Sundays parked on a pew, I had many important ideas about God—none mattering more than the quadratic equation. I *believed* in God, which is not to say that I loved Him, trusted Him, obeyed Him. But everything changed for me one cloudless July day, when, standing beside a lake, I heard the risen Jesus put some important questions to me: What do you want? Where are you headed? Will you follow me?

At sixteen, I had my Damascus road conversion—and I had my Ananias, too. My spiritual fire kindled, a seasoned pastor taught me to fan it into flame. "You'll need good habits," he advised. *Read your Bible ten minutes every day for six months. Pray for five. Share the gospel with someone new every week.* I couldn't have known that his words—and most importantly, the unfailing love of God— would anchor my spiritual life for the better part of three decades: into marriage, into motherhood, even ministry. I have learned that the habits of faith can keep us, even as we keep them.

To understand the gospel is to appreciate habit's proper place. We do not earn our way into God's good graces, and habits will never save us. We don't impress God by our church attendance, our dutiful Bible reading, our fervent prayers. God's love is unearned. It's a gift, writes the apostle Paul in Ephesians chapter 2, "not a result of works, so that no one may boast."

Still, habit plays a central role in the life of a Christian. As the late Dallas Willard once wrote, there's a world of difference between *earning* in the Christian life and *effort*. Darryl Dash's *8 Habits for Growth* has everything to do with the latter. This book invites us to participate in the work God begins in us and completes. It insists that we depend upon divine power—and never presume that spiritual growth is delivered like pizza. A. W. Tozer put it this way, when describing the most important quality of the saints of ages past: "when they felt the inward longing [for God] they *did something about it*. They acquired the lifelong habit of spiritual response."

Darryl Dash is a trusted guide for you as you journey into a life of holiness and the habits of faith. To start, this book is soaked in grace. It's not a "try-harder," "run-faster" book. Darryl understands that we need God's help in forming good habits—that we're quick to resolve and quicker to fail. In fact, one marvelous surprise of this book is that one of the first recommended habits is the regular practice of rest! Importantly, Darryl's book also helps us imagine more than lone-ranger Christianity, reminding us again and again that if we want to walk the way of Jesus, we need the company of fellow pilgrims for the road. Mercifully, this is not a book of nice, wispy ideas, so paper-thin as to see right through them. This is a book offering solid and practical principles necessary for the kind of construction project Jesus describes in one of His parables (see Matt. 7:24–27).

This is a book to build faith that outlasts storms.

I try imagining who might be holding this book in their hands. I pray for you. Maybe some of you have just begun the race of faith.

You're still buoyed by the palpable sense of God's nearness. Maybe some of you have been running a long time. It's the twenty-third mile, and you're weak at the knees. Wherever you are in your journey of faith, whether exhilarated or exhausted, this book can help you to pattern your days, your weeks, your life to become like Jesus and deepen your friendship with Him and His people.

Over the last couple of years, I've been walking alongside a new Christian, a woman who came to faith at fifty. When my friend Esther received God's free gift of grace, offered through Jesus, it was just the beginning. She's thrown herself headlong into the habits Darryl describes in these pages: regular Bible reading, personal prayer, belonging in a local church. In truth, there has been absolutely no magic or mystery to it. She grows like my banana plant: with water and a window.

We can unnecessarily complicate our spiritual lives. In this way, Darryl Dash comes to our rescue with *a simple guide to become like Christ*. This book will likely meet some resistance. You'll wish, as I do, for a quicker, easier road to transformation. But I want to encourage you that habits pay their dividends, not in weeks or months, but in years. What's more, the good news of the gospel is this: *today* is the day of salvation.

Today, you can begin. *Today*, you can begin again.

JEN POLLOCK MICHEL
Author of *A Habit Called Faith*

INTRODUCTION

CONSIDER THIS BOOK AN INVITATION.

First, it's your invitation to grow. This book contains eight habits, which, if built into your everyday life, will change you *forever*.

I'm not into making big promises that don't deliver. I believe that the right small habits, practiced imperfectly, will make a huge difference in your life now and for eternity.

Don't get me wrong. Life will still be crazy. You'll still face time and money pressures. You won't live on a perpetual spiritual high. But you will change, and these changes will be significant. By God's grace, you will see yourself change. You will begin to experience joy and a sense of God's presence in your life even when things get tough.

The power, of course, isn't in the habits themselves. You can practice these habits and completely miss the point. But these habits can lead you to focus daily on what matters most (God) and how He shows up in your ordinary, complicated life.

So please take these habits seriously. Follow the lessons in this book. Be willing to do the hard work of building them into your life. Use them as a guidebook to making small changes that will make an eternal difference.

Second, it's your invitation to help *others* grow. This book is different. My goal is to invite you to not only grow, but to take others along with you. It's not only about you. We are made to grow in relationship, and to respond to Jesus' call to make disciples. (For more on how to help others grow, go to gospelforlife.com/helping-others-grow.)

A *good* way to use this book is to work through it by yourself. A *better* way to use this book is to invite someone to join you. We grow better in community. Think of a friend who may be interested, and invite them to join you. Ask God to bring someone to mind. Check in with each other regularly as you work through this book, meeting at least once per habit to talk about your progress. Use the group questions at the end of each habit to spark discussion.

Perhaps the *best* way to use this book, though, is within the church. I'm a big believer in God's gift of the church. It's where God intends us to grow. If you're a pastor or church leader, use this book as a resource in your ministry as you make disciples who make disciples. See "Using 8 Habits for Growth in Your Church" at gospelforlife.com/using-8-habits for some ideas.

SET YOUR PACE

The aim of this book is simple: to help you develop eight habits that are easy and yet will make a big difference for the rest of your life.

My goal *isn't* that you complete the book. My goal is much bigger: that you integrate the habits I outline in this book for the rest of your life. I'm much more concerned that you take your time and work through this book at a pace that works for you rather than rushing through to get things done.

Each habit contains six lessons and six sets of questions. Here are three options for going through this book.

- **Option A (Eight Weeks):** You could devote a week to each habit, reading the lesson and answering the questions on the same day (taking Sundays off). This approach will allow you to complete the book in eight weeks. I find that few people drop out over eight weeks, although it's more difficult to build and sustain eight habits at this pace.

- **Option B (Sixteen Weeks):** Devote two weeks to each habit, reading the lesson one day and answering the questions on alternate days (taking Sundays off). This will allow you to complete the book in sixteen weeks. Some people drop off with a longer time period, but the extra time allows you to spend more time building each habit before moving on to the next one.

- **Option C (Choose Your Own Adventure):** A final approach is to go at your own pace. Who cares how long it takes? What really matters is that you build the habits and sustain them. If you're not in a rush, if your life is busy, or if you're working with competing schedules in your group, this may be the way to go.

There's no wrong way to use this book. Again, my goal is that you build the eight habits, not that you meet some arbitrary deadline. Find what works for you and adapt this material however you'd like.

HOW TO USE THIS BOOK

I've given you some options for working through this material. But really, I don't care how long or how short it takes you. Your goal isn't simply to complete a workbook. **My desire is that you build the habits described in this book—simple, achievable habits— and practice them for the rest of your life.**

You can work through this book in a few ways.

One way is to dabble at it. I've done this: picked up a book, glanced at the lessons without actually doing them. Usually I lose interest in the book and toss it aside at some point.

I get it. You have limited time and can't commit to everything. Feel free to dip into this book and read in any order you'd like. It's a good way to get a sense of what it's all about. If that gives you what you need at this point, that's great. Perhaps you're just kicking the tires to see if this book will be helpful for you or for others.

A second way to use this book is to complete it. Begin at the beginning and work your way to the end. Give it what you can, even if you can't complete it perfectly.

Depending on your circumstances, simply finishing this book may be a huge accomplishment in your life. You may not be able to give this book your complete attention, and that's okay. Do what you can and benefit from it as much as possible. Maybe later you'll be able to come back and work on some of the habits and go deeper.

> **God delights in satisfying us with Himself when we pursue Him, even when we do so imperfectly.**

A final way to use this book is to internalize it. Start at the beginning. Work through every exercise. Take as long as you need. Go over some sections repeatedly. Take the time you need to internalize the habits into your life.

If you choose this option, it will take a bit more effort, but the results will be worth it. Ask for God's help to internalize the lessons in this book and build them into your life. Nobody will do them perfectly, but if we do them consistently, we'll be putting ourselves in the path of God's grace. God delights in satisfying us with Himself when we pursue Him, even when we do so imperfectly.

If you want more information on the thinking behind *8 Habits for Growth*, then check out my earlier book, *How to Grow: Applying the Gospel to All of Your Life*.

I'm excited and honored that you've picked up this book. Please contact me at darryl@gospelforlife.com if you have any questions, or if I can help you. You can also join the online community at members.gospelforlife.com.

God promises that if we seek Him, we will find Him. Let's take Him up on this promise. Let's go seeking, and let's invite others to come along with us.

THE EIGHT HABITS

The eight habits are structured to help you make permanent changes in your behavior. The first habit is designed to help you prepare to make changes. Habits 2 through 6 are designed to help you take action. The final two habits are designed to help you maintain these habits for a lifetime, and to get back on track when you fail.

1. **Make Time.** Set aside at least 10–15 minutes per day to work through this book, and once you're done with this book, to continue practicing these habits.
2. **Rest and Refresh.** Create daily and weekly rhythms of work and rest in your life.
3. **Engage the Bible.** Spend time reading or listening to the Bible each day.
4. **Speak with God.** Spend time each day praying about whatever is going on in your life.
5. **Worship and Belong.** Find a good church, and commit to regularly worshiping with God's people and living in com-

munity with other Christians.

6. **Care for Your Body.** Take action each day to eat, move, and rest well.

7. **Simplify and Prioritize.** Remind yourself of the goal—intimacy with God—and regularly eliminate distractions from that goal.

8. **Go the Distance.** Create and maintain a set of practices (a Rule of Life) that will guide you in your continued growth.

These habits are designed to help you live well. But they'll also benefit others in your life: your family, friends, neighbors, peers, and coworkers. Most importantly, with God's help, they will help you grow closer to God and love Him and others better.

STAGE	HABIT
Prepare	1. Make Time
Act	2. Rest and Refresh
	3. Engage the Bible
	4. Speak with God
	5. Worship and Belong
	6. Care for Your Body
Maintain	7. Simplify and Prioritize
	8. Go the Distance

Tips for *8 Habits for Growth*

1. **Find a friend.** Work on *8 Habits for Growth* with others.

2. **Do the work.** Skimming the lessons is like trying to get stronger by reading about going to the gym. Make practicing the habit your focus and goal each day.

3. **Practice the Clean Slate Policy.** When you get behind, miss a day, or discover what doesn't work for you, wipe the slate clean and start again.

4. **Pursue progress, not perfection.** Consistency matters more than doing it perfectly.

5. **Shrink the challenge.** If you're not practicing the habit, chances are that you've set a goal that's bigger than the time and energy that you have available. Try shrinking your task until you're 90% sure you can do it.

6. **Keep going, even when you don't see progress.** Small habits, maintained over a long period of time, can lead to lasting change.

7. **Take as long as you need.** Don't just complete this book. Aim to build lifelong habits.

8. **Have fun.** Experiment. Be curious. Take the habits seriously, but approach them playfully. Aim to learn about what works for you and what doesn't. Enjoy the process.

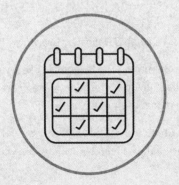

Make Time

HABIT

Make Time. Specifically, make at least 10–15 minutes per day to work through this book, and once you're done, to continue practicing these habits.

ASPIRATION

To make room to develop lasting habits that will help you grow over a lifetime.

CHOOSE YOUR ACTIONS

Choose one or more of the following:

- Pick a time of day when you're alert and not likely to be distracted. Make an appointment with yourself.
- Set an alarm to remind you of your daily appointment.
- Post a reminder of your new habit where you'll see it throughout the day.

Introducing Habit #1:
Make Time

ONE OF THE KEYS to discipleship is to make time.

Welcome to your first official day of *8 Habits for Growth*!

Today, and in the coming days, I'll tell you more about what to expect and why it matters.

But first, it's time to introduce your new habit: **Make Time**. Specifically, make at least 10–15 minutes per day to work through this book, and once you're done, to continue practicing your habits for growth.

Today, and every day for as long as you're working through this book, and then beyond this book as you practice these habits, I want to encourage you to make time.

I know how busy things can get. Work seems to pile up everywhere. There's never enough time to get everything done.

I get it. We're all busy. But there's a problem with busyness.

Busyness can keep us from getting what's most important done.

I wish I could solve the busyness problem, but I can't. I've tried. We all have twenty-four hours, and an abundance of opportunities and responsibilities.

I can't change the challenges you face, but I know this: *Focusing a small amount of your time each day or week to make time for what's most important will add up to big changes in knowing God and becoming who you were made to be.*

Here's what you can do.

- **Decide how much time, realistically, you can spend on this book and these habits each day.** Maybe you are able to get up ten or fifteen minutes earlier, read during your commute or break time, turn off the news, or spend a little less time on social media in the evenings. Or maybe your schedule flows better when you book an appointment with yourself for a longer amount of time a few times a week. Go with what works. The important thing is to decide that time spent working on these habits is essential.

- **Make your decision a reality.** Unfortunately, we don't have a time dispenser. Nobody can give you that, although it would be nice! Whether you grab it, claim it, make it, or give it to yourself as a gift, the key is to take action. Moving from decision to reality always involves an action step.

This time is your commitment to knowing and living the gospel in every part of the one and only life that is uniquely you. Take an action step to protect this time: change the wake-up time on your phone, make a recurring appointment in your calendar, post a reminder, or tell a friend or family member about your decision.

By the way, if you don't know what will work best for you, I encourage you to try the different suggestions mentioned or come up with a few ideas of your own and then experiment to see what works well for you most of the time.

Speaking of what works well, let's take a moment to set healthy expectations. Discovering what works well for you means that sometimes you will discover what does not work for you. If you miss a day or your scheduled appointment time, there's no need for self-criticism. Instead, take a moment to acknowledge the reality, set a new appointment time, and carry on.

I call this the Clean Slate Policy. It's God's policy, and Jesus made it possible, so it's a great rule for life no matter who you are!

HOW DO THESE HABITS WORK?

Here's a little about how *8 Habits for Growth* will work.

In total, I'll give you eight new habits to practice. But don't worry: we'll build them one at a time. The habits are designed to be simple and doable. You get to decide how to apply the habits to your life. Over time, these small habits add up to some big changes in your life.

Each habit has five lessons, five sets of questions, and a review. You can do them over a week or two, or take the time you need. Each lesson or set of questions should take ten or so minutes.

The important thing is to take the time you need to build the habits. I also encourage you to work through this material with others. It's more enjoyable and effective than doing it by yourself.

I want *8 Habits for Growth* to fit into your life. It will take some time; the goal is to make it sustainable. Start small, and then build from there.

- LET'S GET STARTED

This first habit is a time to get settled in. I'll introduce you to the overall approach, and put some important pieces in place.

For today, smile, relax, and drop by the online community at Gospel for Life (members.gospelforlife.com). You can join with others who are working through this material and share your thoughts and your progress.

In the next lesson you get practical and take action with the first habit: Make Time.

I'm glad you've started 8 Habits for Growth, and we can't wait to see what God will do during our time together.

WHAT TO DO TODAY

- **Ask for God's help.** Take a moment to pray. Ask for God's help in making time.
- **Choose your pace.** Take one week to work through each habit (lesson and question each day), or take two weeks per habit (lesson one day; questions the next day), or set your own pace. The choice is yours. I recommend two weeks per habit for most people. This gives you the time you need to really build each habit into your life.
- **Set aside at least 10–15 minutes a day** to work through this material each day to work through this book. Remember: the goal isn't to complete the book, but to build the habits from this book into your life. Start now by making time. It's the foundational step for all that follows.
- **Join with others.** If you're reading this book alone, it's not too late to invite someone else to join you. We grow best with others, not alone.

- **Join the online community** at Gospel for Life (members.gospelforlife.com).

Reflect and Respond

REVIEW

- Busyness can keep us from getting what's most important done.
- Focusing a small amount of your time each day to make time for what's most important will add up to big changes.
- Decide how much time, realistically, you can spend on the habits in this book.
- Make your decision a reality: take an action step.

CONSIDER

- Do you thrive on daily routines? Do you want to add or grow a daily habit?
- Does your weekly rhythm include some days that are busier? Consider your weekly rhythm and identify when you think you will be most successful in making time (for example: 20–30 minutes on Tuesday, Thursday, and Saturday).

DISCUSS

Here are some questions to help you get started. Take the time you need to set yourself up for success.

1. What do you want to get out of *8 Habits for Growth*?
2. How much time can you realistically spend on *8 Habits for Growth* each day?
3. As you look ahead this week, what things could get in the way of you making time?
4. What action step will you take today to make time and stay on track with *8 Habits for Growth*?

Small, Consistent Habits

DON'T BUILD BIG HABITS. Aim for small, consistent habits.

Building habits is hard. Today we're looking at what science can tell us about what works, and what does not work, when we want to create or grow a habit.

TINY HABITS

Do you want to change your behavior? Change your habits. Habits are the unconscious, automatic routines that shape our lives. Charles Duhigg, author of *The Power of Habit*, defines habit as "a behavior that starts as a choice, and then becomes a nearly unconscious pattern."[1] We all have habits, good and bad. Because a large portion of our lives is lived by habit, it's essential that we learn to build good habits that will help us grow.

Habits are powerful, but they're also pretty easy to understand. We want something (desire). We take action to get it (behavior).

And if it works, we may repeat this behavior the next time we face the same situation (prompt). The more we repeat this pattern, the more ingrained the habit becomes.

According to BJ Fogg, a behavior scientist, there's no guesswork involved in building habits. Fogg writes:

> In order to design successful habits and change your behaviors, you should do three things.
>
> - Stop judging yourself.
> - Take your aspirations and break them down into tiny behaviors.
> - Embrace mistakes as discoveries and use them to move forward.[2]

In other words, the place to start is to experiment with small, consistent actions to find what will help us reach our goal. Fogg isn't alone in encouraging us to start small. Saint Basil of Caesarea, who lived almost 1,700 years ago, offered this advice:

> Don't, then, immediately try to force an over-strict discipline on yourself. . . . *It's better to advance in godliness little by little.* So then, withdraw by degrees from this life's indulgences. By slow degrees cast off all your customary bad habits. . . . Master one passion first, and then launch your attack against another. By this method, you will eventually win the victory over them all.[3]

The best way to make changes in your life is to build small, consistent habits.

WHAT THIS MEANS

What does this mean for the eight habits in this book?

Get clear on your goal. Where do you want to grow in your life? What would success look like for you?

Make it easy. Fogg says that it's best not to set a goal to floss all of our teeth. Instead, set a goal to floss one tooth. That behavior is so small that you're likely to do it. You just may decide to floss the rest of them once you've started.

I encourage you to set small goals for the eight habits. Don't be too demanding at first. It's better to take small actions consistently than to take big actions occasionally.

Keep experimenting, and don't give up when you fail. Embrace mistakes. Become a student of your behavior. Learn from what doesn't work. Stay curious. Refuse to get discouraged.

You need more than information and motivation. Don't get me wrong. I will give you information, and I definitely want to motivate you. But we need more than content. We need to translate knowledge and motivation into action.

OVER TO YOU

My advice as we begin? Start small. Be realistic. Expect that things won't always go well. That's okay. Progress is better than perfection.

Anticipate problems. When things don't go well, see if you can shrink the challenge and make it even easier. Make it so small that you can't possibly fail.

When you begin a new habit, it's always a good idea to ask how likely you are to succeed. If you rate yourself lower than a 9/10, then shrink the action. Keep shrinking the action until you rate your likelihood of success at 9/10 or higher.

It's a great idea to relax and to take things slow. We're interested in creating lasting change. In the long run, tiny habits work best.

Don't get discouraged! Christopher Love encourages us: "God not only exactly takes notice of, but also tenderly cherishes and graciously rewards, the smallest beginnings and weakest measures of grace which He works in the hearts of His own people."[4] Small, consistent actions are bigger than we think.

WHAT TO DO TODAY

- **Schedule 10–15 minutes of time each day** to work through this book.
- **Keep experimenting** to find what works best for you.

Reflect and Respond

REVIEW

- **Get specific.** Break down desired outcomes or goals into behaviors.
- **Make it easy.** Ask how you can shrink the behavior so it's easier to do.
- **Keep experimenting.** Treat mistakes as learning experiences.

CONSIDER

- Think of an action or behavior that was beneficial or uplifting and was easy to do. What did you do? Who were you with? Where were you? At what time of day or night? What prompted or encouraged you?
- Think of a recent task or behavior that was difficult for you. What did you do? Who were you with? Where were you? At what time of day or night? What made it difficult?
- What kinds of things make an action easier for you? What makes it harder? Be patient. Experiment with different approaches to building new habits in your life.

DISCUSS

Use these questions to move yourself forward. Take the time you need to learn a little more about yourself and grow your habit of making time.

1. How is the making time habit working for you?
2. What would it look like if you had a little more success with this habit?
3. How can you shrink this habit so that it works even better for you?
4. What's one good thing about this habit for you?
5. How will you remind yourself to practice this habit every day?

HABIT 1, LESSON 3

Why Are You Here?

TAKE THE TIME TO EXPLORE your motivations and goals.

You've started working through this book. You've decided to bite the bullet and take steps to grow over these next few weeks.

You may be here for any number of reasons. So I want to ask you two personal questions. What's your motivation? And what are your goals?

FIND YOUR MOTIVATION

It's possible that you started this book only because someone invited you. But I'm guessing that you have a desire to grow spiritually.

What motivates you to grow spiritually? What areas of dissatisfaction do you sense in your life right now? What's your big "why" for wanting to apply the gospel to every part of your life?

Is there a reason, right now, that you're making your growth a priority?

FIND YOUR GOALS

In just a few weeks, if you keep going, you'll have finished this book. You'll have read forty lessons, answered numerous questions, and practiced eight habits. I hope you'll also have enjoyed working through this book alone or, even better, with others.

This isn't a long time, but it's long enough to make meaningful progress. When you finish the last lesson, how do you hope that your life has changed?

For now, don't worry about being practical. Picture the future you. Where do you want to be? How do you want to feel? How will your life have changed? Try to describe your hopes and goals in as much detail as possible.

- I want to be . . .
- I want to feel . . .
- I want to change . . .

Don't worry about coming up with the perfect answers. It's sometimes hard to understand our own motivations and goals. Just make your best attempt.

WHAT TO DO TODAY

- **Look ahead** to your plans for tomorrow.
- **Decide when and where** you will practice your habit of making time.
- **Think about your motivations and goals:** Why do you really want to grow? How will your life have changed at the end of this book?
- **Keep making at least 10–15 minutes per day** to work through this book.

Reflect and Respond

REVIEW

- **Find your motivation**
- **Find your goals**

CONSIDER

- As you look at your life, where are you experiencing joy and satisfaction?
- Where are you dissatisfied?
- Is there a reason, right now, that you've made *8 Habits for Growth* a priority?

Don't worry about coming up with the perfect answers. It's sometimes hard to understand our own motivations and goals. Just make your best attempt.

DISCUSS

These are some of the most important questions for you to answer. Later in the book we'll come back to them.

Take the time to think about them as honestly as you can.

1. What's your big "why" for wanting to apply the gospel to every part of your life?
2. Why is (your previous answer) important to you?
3. What's the real challenge here for you?
4. Picture the "future you." Describe your hopes and goals in as much detail as possible.

   I want to be . . .
   I want to feel . . .
   I want to change . . .

WHAT'S COMING UP

Keep practicing your habit of making time:

- Take a few minutes today or tomorrow to look ahead at your plans and commitments for the coming week.
- Decide where and when you will practice this habit each day.
- Ask yourself if you need to shrink the habit.
- Create reminders of your habit to increase your chances of success.

Next, we'll go deeper with the role of the heart in how we change.

The End Game

REAL CHANGE HAPPENS at the level of the heart.

How do people change? Entire books have been written to answer this question.

People need knowledge to change, but knowledge isn't enough. We all know we should eat more vegetables, but we don't always do it. Reading books, attending classes, and learning new things are helpful, but they don't always change our lives.

Knowledge isn't enough. Neither is behavior change. We can try to change our actions for a while, but behavior is just the tip of the iceberg. Only a small percentage of our behavior is the outcome of conscious, deliberate choices. The rest of our actions and behaviors come from a much deeper place.

Many of our efforts to change focus on knowledge and behavior, and don't really work over the long term. We need to go a lot deeper if we want to change.

THE IMPORTANCE OF THE HEART

Real change happens at the deepest possible level. It happens in the heart.

The Bible contains an important truth:

Above all else, guard your heart,
for everything you do flows from it.
(Prov. 4:23 NIV)

> **Real change happens at the deepest possible level. It happens in the heart.**

In Scripture, the heart represents the inner being of a person. It's more than just the mind or actions. It's the control center of our lives. According to the verse, everything we do comes out of our heart.

We often try to change our actions, thoughts, and feelings. God wants to go deeper and change us at the level of the heart, the source of all our behaviors.

Growth involves knowledge and action, but it goes much deeper. Real change happens at the level of the heart.

WHAT DO YOU WANT?

Jesus asked two of His disciples a penetrating question: "What do you want me to do for you?" (Mark 10:36). Their answer revealed a misshapen desire: they wanted to sit at Jesus' left and right hand, places of prominence. Jesus didn't just deal with their behaviors. He probed their desires, and then showed them how their desires could change to be more like His.

In the same passage, Jesus repeated the same question to a blind man named Bartimaeus. This time, the answer to Jesus' question revealed a legitimate desire: "Rabbi, let me recover my sight" (Mark 10:51). Jesus answered his request and healed him.

"What do you want me to do for you?" What an insightful question. Our desires and longings determine everything about us. They shape our actions and behaviors, sometimes without us even knowing it. The Christian life involves asking God to change what we want. It's praying something like this: "Father, teach me to want rightly, and help me to live in obedience to those right desires."[5]

We need to aim for more than knowledge and actions. We need to experience change at the deepest level: in the heart.

Discipleship is about growing as a disciple of Jesus in every area of life. What comes to mind when you think of a mature Christian disciple? The goal of discipleship may surprise you.

Sam Storms, a pastor in Oklahoma, explains:

> God is most glorified in us when we are most happy and delighted and satisfied in Him. . .
>
> The single most important principle I ever discovered is this: the goal or purpose of the Christian is precisely the pursuit of happiness—in God. The reason for this is that there is no greater way to glorify God than to find in Him the happiness that my soul so desperately craves.[6]

Jesus told us that the greatest command is to love God with all our heart, soul, mind, and strength (Mark 12:30). David, the psalmist, modeled this when he wrote:

> As a deer pants for flowing streams,
>   so pants my soul for you, O God.
> My soul thirsts for God,
>   for the living God.
> (Ps. 42:1–2)

The goal of discipleship is happiness, joy, delight, satisfaction, and intimacy with God. The holiest person you will ever meet is also the happiest person you'll ever meet.

That's the kind of Christian maturity all of us can get behind.

> **The goal of discipleship is happiness, joy, delight, satisfaction, and intimacy with God.**

THE STARTING PLACE

Christianity isn't about us changing ourselves. It's about God giving us a new heart. God promises to remove our heart of stone and give us a heart of flesh (Ezek. 36:26).

God is holy. We are sinful. Something is wrong with all of us: our hearts are dead. We can't fix that problem ourselves. Nothing we can do by ourselves can change the condition of our hearts. God must change us.

God has acted through Jesus to rescue us, change us, and bring us into relationship with Him. He promises to change our hearts.

God made you to desire Him. He made you for relationship with Him. The most important thing you can do to change is to stop living life on your own terms and to trust in Jesus. He will change you at the level of your heart, and you'll never be the same.

If you haven't already done so, this is the place to start. If you're working through this book with someone else, talk to them about what this means. Don't go further until you've settled the issue of God giving you a new heart.

THE PATH TO CHANGE

God changes us at a fundamental level when we trust in Jesus. He changes us from the inside out. We continue to grow as we learn to delight in Him.

If we want to deepen the transformation in our hearts, fight sin, and grow in grace, then this is the path. Revel in the beauty and splendor of God, and become happy in Him.

Sam Storms writes:

> The only thing that will ultimately break the power of sin is passion for Jesus. The only thing that will guard me from being entrapped by sin is being entranced by Jesus. In other words, the key to holiness is falling in love![7]

This is the ultimate goal of discipleship: to find our happiness in God.

WHAT TO DO TODAY

- **Celebrate your success** today with making time.
- **If you haven't already done so, ask God to give you a new heart.** If you're going through this book with someone, talk to them about what this means. Turn from self-reliance to Jesus, and ask Him to change you from the inside out.
- **Look ahead** to your plans for tomorrow and consider what challenges you may face in this habit of making time. Do you need to shrink the habit? Or do you need a bigger challenge? Decide what will work for you.
- **Commit** to when and where you will practice your habit of making 10–15 minutes a day to work through this material.

Reflect and Respond

REVIEW

- Efforts to change that focus on knowledge and behavior often fail in the long term.
- Real change happens in the heart. We are what we want.
- God changes us by giving us new hearts.
- The goal or purpose of the Christian is the pursuit of happiness in God.[8]

CONSIDER

How is making time working for you?

If it's not working the way you want it to, think about what's getting in your way. What could you do to

- shrink the habit?
- change the trigger?
- get encouragement from a friend, mentor, or coach?
- pursue happiness in God?

DISCUSS

1. The goal of discipleship is happiness in God. How is this different from the way you usually think about discipleship?
2. George Müller said, "The first great and primary business to which I ought to attend every day was, to get my soul to be happy in the Lord."[9] What steps can you take today to make your soul happy in God?

Begin Where You Are

TO REACH OUR GOAL, we need to know our starting point.

You get in your car and fire up the GPS. You know where you want to go. Before you can begin your journey, though, the GPS has to know where you are now.

It's a rule in life: to go from here to there, you need to know where you are now, and where you'd ultimately like to be.

GROWTH STAGES

Before you decide on your destination, it's helpful to figure out where you are now in your relationship with God.

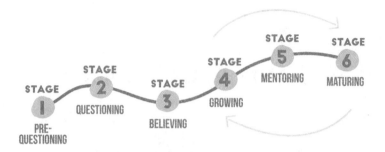

- The **Pre-Questioning** may not believe in God, or they may believe in a different god from the God revealed in Scripture. They aren't really interested in Jesus and His message.
- The **Questioning** don't know much about Jesus, but are open.
- The **Believing** identify as Christian. Some believe intellectually, but have not had a life-changing encounter with Jesus. Others have experienced forgiveness and freedom from sin and shame through Christ's death and resurrection.
- The **Growing** show evidence of a relationship with Jesus Christ. They are growing in their love for God, have joined a church community, and are learning the basics of the faith.
- The **Mentoring** are growing in love, faith, and obedience, and are helping others to grow.
- The **Maturing** don't often think much of themselves. They walk with a limp as they share the beauty of God's faithful love from their lives.

We need different things at each stage:

- The **Pre-Questioning** need stimulating conversations, genuine friendships with Christians, and the opportunity to see the Christian faith lived out.

- The **Questioning** can grow by learning the story of Christianity, exploring the Bible, and seeing the Christian faith lived out in community.
- The **Believing** can grow by learning the basics of Christianity, reading the Bible, praying, and learning from other Christians.
- The **Growing** can grow by learning and applying the gospel to everyday life, developing habits of grace, and helping others progress through the stages.
- The **Mentoring** can grow by looking for faithful people, entrusting the gospel to them, and helping them become disciple-makers.
- The **Maturing** can continue to grow by sharing their lives with others, and by drawing even closer to Christ.[10]

Of course, life isn't simple, and we may not fit neatly into a particular stage. It's still a good idea to know where we are in the process, so that we know what step we need to take.

Maturity is a process. No matter what stage we're in, we can take the next step.

WHAT TO DO TODAY

- **Review the Growth Stages** and estimate your spiritual stage. You can also take an online assessment at https://gospelforlife.com/stages/.
- **Review what and who you need** for growth at your stage.
- **Look ahead at your plans for tomorrow.** Decide where and when you will continue your habit of making time.

Reflect and Respond

REVIEW

Before you begin, determine where you are:

- **Stage 1, Pre-Questioning**
- **Stage 2, Questioning**
- **Stage 3, Believing**
- **Stage 4, Growing**
- **Stage 5, Mentoring**
- **Stage 6, Maturing**

CONSIDER

- Life isn't simple so we may not fit neatly into a particular stage.
- There's often a gap between where we are in our head (what we know) and where we are in reality (what we actually do). If you haven't already done so, consider taking the self-assessment quiz at https://gospelforlife.com/stages/.

DISCUSS

1. What's your stage (Pre-Questioning, Questioning, Believing, Growing, Mentoring, or Maturing)?
2. What do you need to continue to grow?
3. Who do you need to help you continue to grow?

HABIT #1:
MAKE TIME

Review

CONGRATULATIONS! You completed Habit 1 (Make Time).

In this first habit, we focused on the preparation habit—making time—which is foundational for the other habits in this book.

- We learned about the power of small, consistent habits.
- We talked about the importance of focusing on our hearts, rather than just getting more knowledge or focusing on behavior.
- We focused on the starting point: that we must ask God to give us new hearts. When we turn away from living life on our own terms and trust in Jesus, He promises to change us from the inside out.
- We defined the end goal of Christian maturity: happiness in God.
- We assessed where we are now, and what steps we can take next.

If you're working through this book with others, check in and share what you've learned, the answers to some of your questions, and where you struggled.

Be encouraged. You've come this far. You're building a habit of making time. Way to go! Keep going, even if it hasn't been perfect.

RESOURCES

Visit gospelforlife.com/make-time for resources on this habit.

EVALUATION

1. What went well in Habit 1 (Make Time)?
2. What have you learned?
3. Where have you struggled?
4. What can you do today to continue to build this habit?

WHAT TO DO TODAY

- **Think about what's worked so far** as you've progressed through this book.
- If you're working through this book with others, **check in with them** to see how they are doing.
- **Review this habit**, and highlight anything that sticks out to you.
- **Celebrate successes, even when they're small.**
- **Thank God for His work in you** as you practiced this habit.

Group Discussion Questions

READ PHILIPPIANS 3:7–11.

1. Paul says that knowing Jesus is better than anything else in his life (3:7–8). Why do you think that it's so important for us to know Jesus?

2. Paul makes it clear that he's not trusting in his own righteousness but in the righteousness that comes through faith in Christ (3:9). We don't have enough righteousness of our own; we need God to help us. Why is our righteousness not enough? Do you find yourself resisting or running toward the clean slate that Jesus offers you in your daily growth?

3. Paul's whole goal is to know Jesus (3:10). In Habit 1, we've talked about the importance of happiness, joy, delight, satisfaction, and intimacy with God. How is this different from how you normally think of spiritual growth?

4. How have you been doing in making time (at least 10–15 minutes each day) to work through this material? What successes can you celebrate? How can you shrink or grow the challenge to make this habit work better for you?

5. How do you feel about small, consistent habits? Do you have any examples in your life of building habits like these?

6. What questions do you have about any of the material we've covered so far?

Rest and Refresh

HABIT

Rest. Specifically, build a rhythm of work and rest into your life on a daily and weekly basis.

ASPIRATION

To live according to how our Creator designed us to function, enjoying both physical and spiritual rest.

CHOOSE YOUR ACTIONS

Choose one or more of the following:

- Pick a daily action (taking a nap or bath, going for a walk, reading a book) that brings you rest.
- Brainstorm a list of activities that refresh you and make you feel more alive.
- Make a list of activities that are pseudo-rest, that look restful but leave you drained (e.g., excessive social media scrolling, playing video games for too long, or binge-watching shows).
- Pick a recurring date for a full-day Sabbath, and put it on the calendar.

Introducing Habit #2:
Rest and Refresh

WE WERE MADE TO PRACTICE rhythms of work and rest.

Welcome to Habit 2.

Continue to practice Habit 1. Continue to make time every day to do your lessons, even if it's only ten or fifteen minutes every day.

We want you to also add a new habit starting this week: rest.

This could be as simple as taking five or ten minutes to read a book, go for a walk, or to take a nap. If you want a bigger challenge, take five or ten minutes to plan for an entire day of rest—a Sabbath—this week. Start small, and build toward that goal.

Find something that works for you. Make it as big or small as you need.

MADE FOR WORK AND REST

We're busy. We face an unending stream of emails, tasks, and responsibilities.

On one hand, this is good. God made us for meaningful work. If you are getting stuff done, that's a good thing.

The problem is that some of us are better at working than resting. We need both.

I won't tell you to quit your job and join a monastery. God has called and gifted you for His purposes, and I want you to throw yourself at making the most of the opportunities that He gives you.

But we also need to rest. Don't wait until the work is done. Make the decision to stop and to deliberately set aside all obligations.

Create a rhythm of work and rest.

HOW TO REST

Later in this habit, we will look at why rest is important. Today, let's talk about how to rest.

Rest isn't a passive activity.

Rest is choosing to pursue activities that renew and refresh you. Here are some ideas to try as you build a habit of rest:

- **Disengage**. Make a deliberate decision to stop work, even though there's more work to do. The work will still be there when you're done resting.
- **Turn off the screens**. Turn the phones, tablets, and computers off. We rarely feel recharged after spending time online, binging on Netflix, or watching television. If you spend a lot of time using technology, look for a low-tech way to recharge.
- **Read a book**. Find a book that you'd like to read for no practical reason, except that it brings you enjoyment.
- **Go for a walk**. Lace up your shoes, and explore your neighborhood.

- **Play**. Get a board game or a basketball and have some fun. In his book *The Well-Played Life*, Leonard Sweet writes, "The older we get, the more we need *allowance* and *permission* to play, and the more we need instruction on *how* to play."[1]
- **Sleep**. Take a nap, or go to bed early.
- **Find a hobby**. Think about a hobby that you used to enjoy, and try it again.
- **Contact a friend**. Spend some time on the phone. Even better, go out for coffee or some food.

Be careful of activities that look like rest, but don't leave you feeling recharged. For instance, Netflix and social media help us escape from work and responsibilities, but they don't leave us feeling more alive. Pursue activities that awaken and refresh you. Examples may include walks, reading, sports, visiting with friends, or pursuing hobbies. Any action that is enjoyable and isn't an obligation qualifies as rest. Theologian J. I. Packer advises us to "choose the leisure activities that bring us closest to God, to people, to beauty, and to all that ennobles."[2]

The key is to release yourself from all obligations and to find something that renews you. Start by doing this for a small amount of time each day. As you get better at rest, we encourage you to set a goal of one day of rest every week.

Whether for a few minutes, a few hours, or an entire day, release yourself from all obligations. Play, recharge, connect with friends, enjoy God's presence, and pursue activities that renew you.

Consider these thoughts on God's idea of rest (Sabbath) from Reggie McNeal:

Remember, Sabbath is a gift to us from God. Accept his invitation. You can relax in his presence because he is safe to share your life with. More than anything else, he just wants the time to be with you. Unfettered and unbusy time to enjoy you, to show you his love. Time to make you a champion at living.[3]

WHAT TO DO TODAY

- **Look for something that will refresh you.** Make time for rest today. Work on being fully present and alive. Celebrate God's presence with you, and thank Him for His goodness and care. Allow your heart to rest. Look for anxieties that come up, especially during your rest time, and hand them over to God for the day.

- **After you have rested,** look ahead at your plans for this week and decide where and when you will make time for your new habits.

Reflect and Respond

REVIEW

- We were made to live in a rhythm of work and rest.
- God made us for meaningful work, but we also need to rest.
- Rest is choosing to pursue activities that renew and refresh you.

5 Tips to Rest Well

1. Disengage and stop working, even though there's more work to do.
2. Release yourself from all obligations.
3. Turn off the screens.
4. Choose activities that recharge you rather than activities that look like rest but only extend weariness.
5. Experiment to find what brings you renewal.

CONSIDER

- Are you renewed by gathering with a large group of people, spending time with one or two close friends, or by time completely on your own?
- What are you doing when you feel closest to God?

DISCUSS

1. What activities do you find renewing?
2. What action will you take to rest, even for a few minutes, today?

HABIT 2, LESSON 2

Why Rest?

GOD COMMANDS REST. Jesus promises rest. We need rest.

> **"If we do not regularly quit work for one day a week we take ourselves far too seriously."**
> **(Eugene Peterson)**[4]

You may be surprised that the second habit is rest. Why not focus on reading the Bible or prayer?

Don't worry. We'll get to those topics. But until we begin to address the issue of rest, it's difficult to make progress in other areas.

Sometimes, rest comes first.

HURRY SICKNESS

Many of us suffer from hurry sickness. We rush through our days and never have enough time to get everything done.

Dr. Suzanne Koven, who practices internal medicine at Massachusetts General Hospital, writes:

> In the past few years, I've observed an epidemic of sorts: patient after patient suffering from the same condition. The symptoms of this condition include fatigue, irritability, insomnia, anxiety, headaches, heartburn, bowel disturbances, back pain, and weight gain. There are no blood tests or X-rays diagnostic of this condition, and yet it's easy to recognize. The condition is excessive busyness.[5]

When hurry becomes our default, our relationships begin to suffer. We begin to skim through life. The problem goes deeper than our schedule. As Philip Nation notes, "The hurry that we inflict upon ourselves is not from a chaotic schedule. Hurry is a sign of a chaotic heart."[6]

Hurry affects our relationships and souls. Rest helps to break the pattern of busyness, and is essential for physical, relational, and spiritual health.

THREE REASONS TO REST

The Bible gives us three good reasons to rest.

God Commands Rest

In the creation week, God rested. God instituted a pattern of work and rest that continues today. It's built into the very fabric of creation, pointing to the ultimate rest that He intends for us to enjoy one day.

When God gave His people the law, He included a commandment to rest. He didn't give us this command to burden us. He gave this command out of love.[7]

While scholars debate whether this applies to us today, I agree with Christopher Ash: "Even if the Sabbath is no longer an old-covenant religious obligation, we are simply foolish to behave as though we no longer need a day off each week."[8]

Put simply, God created us to function well when we work and rest.

Jesus Promises Rest

Jesus said,

"Come to me, all who labor and are heavy laden, and I will give you rest. Take my yoke upon you, and learn from me, for I am gentle and lowly in heart, and you will find rest for your souls. For my yoke is easy, and my burden is light." (Matt. 11:28–30)

Rest isn't just the absence of work. Jesus pictures us working, except with one difference: we become yoked, like oxen, with Him. Jesus calls us to give up self-reliance and to be refreshed as we rely on Him. He speaks not just about physical rest but rest for our *souls*. Our relationship with Jesus allows us to move from self-reliance to restful dependence on God.

We Need Rest

Scripture teaches that we are dust (Gen. 3:19). Unlike God, we tire. We are finite creatures. We need sleep and refreshment. John Piper reminds us:

Sleep is a daily reminder from God that we are not God. . . . Once a day God sends us to bed like patients with a sickness. The sickness is a chronic tendency to think we are in control and that our work is indispensable. To cure us of this disease God turns us into helpless sacks of sand once a day.[9]

Rest teaches us about our limits and leads us to rely on God.

WHAT TO DO TODAY

- **Practice your new habit:**
  - What type of rest do you need most today?
  - Are you confident you are able to get the rest you need today? If not, how can you start small?
  - Experiment with different restful activities. Play.
  - Try to discover what's restful for you.
- **Intentionally make time for rest in your life.**

Reflect and Respond

REVIEW

Three reasons to rest:

1. **God commands rest.** God created us to function well when we work and rest.
2. **Jesus promises rest.** Our relationship with Jesus allows us to move from self-reliance to restful dependence in Him.
3. **We need rest.** Sleep reminds us about our limits and leads us to move from self-reliance to rely on God each day.

CONSIDER

- When you take time for rest, what negative thoughts, fears, or anxieties come to your mind?
- Offer yourself and your time to God's design and ask Him to provide what is needed for you to rest.

DISCUSS

1. Which reason for rest is most compelling for you?
   - God commands rest.
   - Jesus promises rest.
   - I need rest.
2. A. J. Swobada writes, "The Sabbath is a gift we do not know how to receive. In a world of doing, going, and producing, we have no use for a gift that invites us to stop."[10] Why do you think we have such a hard time receiving this gift?
3. What gets in the way of rest for you?
4. What action will you take to rest, even for a few minutes, today?

HABIT 2, LESSON 3

24/6

REST TIME ISN'T WASTED TIME.

A wagon train made its way from St. Louis to Oregon. Its members were Christians. They traveled for six days and then rested on the seventh.

Some grew concerned about the coming winter. They argued that they wouldn't reach their destination before the coming snow. They suggested that they skip their Sabbath breaks, and travel seven days a week.

When they couldn't agree, the wagon train split into two. One traveled six days a week and rested; the other traveled seven days a week without rest.

Guess which group arrived first? The ones who rested a day a week. The people and horses were so refreshed by their occasional break that they traveled with more vigor and energy the other days of the week.[11]

YOU DON'T LOSE THE TIME YOU REST

Resting a day a week is a big deal. It adds up to fifty-two days a year, or eleven years over the average lifespan. That seems like a lot of time to lose to rest.

According to Matthew Sleeth, a former emergency room doctor and hospital chief of staff, we lose more if we don't take a day off every week to rest. We miss out on three things we need most: *rest, renewal,* and *reverence*:

- rest, not just from our work, but "from the tyranny of the urgent, the staggering precipice of eternity, and the mundane workweek";
- renewal, as we engage in activities that refresh and energize us;
- reverence, as we catch a glimpse of the divine.[12]

Ironically, taking the time to rest may not cost us anything. It looks like it costs us eleven years over our lifetime. But some evidence shows that people who live longer lives seem to take more time off.

"In other words, the number of extra years they live is roughly equivalent to the number of days they spend in Sabbath keeping," writes Sleeth. "It may be coincidence, but the Bible hints at a cause-and-effect relationship between keeping the Sabbath and living a long life. Living 24/7 is life draining; living 24/6 is life-giving."[13]

The benefits of living 24/6 are profound. When we rest for a day a week, it may seem like we lose time, but we don't. We gain rest, renewal, and reverence.

OVER TO YOU

I know that it's not easy to live 24/6. Sleeth says, "If we wish to have a weekly day of rest, it will no longer happen as a societal default. It will happen only as a result of a conscious choice."[14]

For today, it may not be easy, but I encourage you to:

1. **Take a few minutes to do something restful or renewing.** It doesn't have to be perfect. Try something new—or not! You decide.

2. **Think about taking one day off this week.** If taking a full day seems overwhelming, shrink the challenge. Go for half a day, or an hour or two. Plan to do something that energizes and refreshes you. Throw out your task list. Look for God. Play. You may find that you get more back from your time off than you lose.

3. **Have fun!** Don't turn rest into work. Approach your rest with a playful attitude.

Reflect and Respond

REVIEW

Through Sabbath-keeping we gain:

- Rest
- Renewal
- Reverence

CONSIDER

Sometimes we're scared to rest because we're afraid that we won't get as much done. But rest may give us the perspective we need to make better choices and replenish us for the work God gives us to do.

- Can you identify any fears you experience about building more rest and Sabbath into your life?
- How might rest and Sabbath help you lead a more meaningful life?

DISCUSS

1. How do you feel about taking a full or partial day off every week?
   - Overwhelmed
   - Ambivalent
   - I've got this
2. What action will you take to rest today?

Interlude: Sabbath

IS TODAY YOUR SABBATH? Great! Then this bonus lesson is for you.

If it isn't your Sabbath, bookmark this page and return to it the next time you plan on taking a full day of rest.

GOD'S GIFT OF REST

Imagine being given an extra ten weeks of vacation each year. Think about how you'd be able to use that time to renew yourself and do things that you love.

God has given us that amount of rest each year: fifty-two days in which we can lay aside all obligations and simply enjoy Him and His gifts. This Sabbath pattern goes right back to creation (Gen. 2:2–3), and was commanded by God in the longest of the Ten Commandments (Ex. 20:8–11).

Theologians debate whether Sabbath is still commanded for believers today because of passages like Colossians 2:16–17. But I believe the Sabbath principle still exists as a reminder of our limits and as a gracious gift for us to enjoy. As Justin Huffman writes:

> Like having to sleep every night to stay healthy, we need a weekly rest for our body and mind and spirit. We need a regular reminder to pull aside from the cares and obligation of our daily lives and instead focus on Christ, his Word, and the rest we have in him.[15]

HOW TO TAKE A SABBATH

Here are some guidelines I've found helpful on how to take a Sabbath.

1. **Pick a day.** Israel celebrated Sabbath on the seventh day (sundown on Friday to sundown on Saturday). Some think that the early church shifted this day to Sunday, or the Lord's Day (Rev. 1:10). Because I pastor on Sundays, I've chosen to take Fridays as my weekly Sabbath. Pick the day that works best in the rhythms of your life.

2. **Stop working.** "Six days you shall labor, and do all your work, but the seventh day is a Sabbath to the LORD your God. On it you shall not do any work . . ." (Ex. 20:9–10). Sabbath is not a chore day. It's a day to stop doing whatever it is that we do the other six days. If it feels like work, I try not to do it on my weekly Sabbath. My main rule: no obligations! (Disclaimer: Some of us, like parents of young children, may not be able to escape *all* obligations.)

3. **Engage in activities that refresh you.** John Piper advises, "Do things on the Lord's day that refresh us for his service, intellectually, physically and spiritually. So if you sit at your desk all week, you should probably walk or ride a bike on Sunday. And if you work on the farm, breaking your back all week (which is

what they did in the Old Testament), then sit down and take a long nap on Sunday."[16] Build a list of things that recharge you, and do those. And also build a list of activities that look restful but aren't (such as scrolling on social media), and avoid them. Make the day special.

4. **Pursue God.** Reorient yourself. You're more than what you do. God made you not just for work, but for relationship with Him and others. Focus on something beyond yourself and your work. Remember: God made you to delight in Him. He loves you. Keep the day holy by engaging in activities that draw you closer to Him, that remind you of His presence, and allow you to enjoy the pleasure of His love.

WHAT TO DO TODAY

Make time to increase your rest and wholeheartedness in Jesus.
What can you do to set aside work, hurry-sickness, obligations, and stress for some intentional time of renewal, joy, and play? Finish your time by giving thanks to God for His generous provision of rest today.

Is today mostly a Sabbath, but you still have to do some work? I love that you're "shrinking the challenge." Do what you can to rest today, and keep making progress toward a full, weekly Sabbath rest.

Encourage one another. Share your past or current experiences of rest and Sabbath with your friends and family, and with the online community at members.gospelforlife.com.

MAKING IT WORK FOR YOU

If taking an entire day is overwhelming, start with a smaller period of time.

Don't expect perfection. Approach your Sabbath time as an experiment in finding rest and joy in God, not as an obligation.

If a Rest Day (or part day) is new for you, expect it to disrupt your patterns of behavior and rhythms. This may leave you with any number of feelings: energized, stressed, ambivalent, or unconvinced. There's no "right" experience—what's most important is to notice and name what you feel, lay it openly before God, and ask Him to do more of His good work in your heart, mind, soul, and body.

If keeping a Sabbath day is a long-practiced habit for you, ask the Holy Spirit to reveal any behaviors or beliefs that may interfere with the rest that God desires for you today. Encourage other believers by sharing your experiences of God's rest.

HABIT 2, LESSON 4

Wholehearted

WE DON'T JUST NEED REST. We need wholeheartedness.

How are you doing with Habit 2?

If you are doing well, congratulations. Keep experimenting with what recharges and renews you. Whether you're resting for ten or fifteen minutes a day, keep building your capacity to rest.

If you're struggling, be patient. Rest is like a muscle that we need to develop. Ironically, resting is hard work. Keep experimenting. When you face resistance, gently notice what is behind that resistance. Rather than judging, just notice.

We're all different. Find what works for you, and take small actions to build your resting capacity.

THE ANTIDOTE TO EXHAUSTION

David Whyte, a poet, asked his friend David Steindl-Rast about exhaustion.

"You know that the antidote to exhaustion is not necessarily rest?" responded Steindl-Rast.

Whyte froze in his tracks. "The antidote to exhaustion is not necessarily rest? What is it, then?"

His friend responded, "The antidote to exhaustion is whole-heartedness."[17]

In his book *Wholeheartedness*, Chuck DeGroat explains how this exchange affected him:

> My own hypocrisy was exposed. I was living the divided life. . . . I wasn't wholehearted. And that prevented me from finding any real and deep rest.
>
> True rest was something I didn't know how to do. I could stop my usual activities. I could watch a football game on a Sunday afternoon. I could even take a nap. But these things could not and would not stop the frenzied inner activity that continued incessantly. In my divided soul, true "rest" didn't have a fighting chance.[18]

When we feel scattered, anxious, and busy, we don't just need physical rest. We need wholeheartedness.

BECOMING WHOLEHEARTED

There's no shortcut to becoming wholehearted, but there are some steps we can take.

As you rest, pay attention to areas of your life where you aren't experiencing rest. What areas of your life seem out of sync with your deepest self? What parts of your life feel shut off from God?

Paying attention to these areas is an important first step. Look for the ways that you may be living with a divided heart, and begin to bring these areas to God. Ask Him to bring these areas into alignment with the rest of your life, and thank God that He knows everything about you.

Wholeheartedness is a lifelong journey, and it is the path to finding rest in the deepest parts of our souls.

WHAT TO DO TODAY

1. **Continue to look for ways to practice your rest habit.** Take a few minutes to do something restful today.
2. **Put a date on your calendar** for your next Sabbath.
3. **Pray about the areas of your life where you don't feel wholehearted.** Ask a friend to pray with you. Ask God to bring greater wholeness into your life.

Reflect and Respond

REVIEW

Real and deep rest requires that we become wholehearted. We don't just need physical rest; we need rest for our souls.

CONSIDER

- In what areas of your life are you not experiencing rest?
- What areas of your life seem out of sync with your deepest self?
- What parts of your life feel shut off from God?
- Do you see any ways that you may be living with a divided heart? If so, bring these areas to God. Ask Him to bring these areas into alignment with the rest of your life.
- Thank God that He knows and loves every part of you—body, heart, mind, and soul.

DISCUSS

What are some areas in your life in which you don't feel wholehearted? Write them down, or share them with a friend.

True Rest

TRUE REST IS FINDING OUR SECURITY in being known and loved by God.

Hopefully you're enjoying developing a habit of rest.

As you've probably discovered, making rest a habit is hard work. It's a skill that we can develop with time. It requires courage and intentionality.

As long as we're alive, we'll need to continue to develop the skill of resting. We encourage you to practice getting rest every day. For at least a few minutes, forget about your obligations, and really enjoy all that God has given you.

Then, once a week, enjoy a full day of rest. Release yourself from all obligations and find leisure activities that bring you closer to God, people, beauty, and activities that make you feel alive.

If a day a week is too much, start with less and build to a full day. You'll begin to enjoy uncluttered time to enjoy God, and get a sense of what He's doing in your life. You'll enjoy not just doing, but being.

ENTERING GOD'S REST

The Bible promises the best kind of rest for all of God's people:

> So then, there remains a Sabbath rest for the people of God, for whoever has entered God's rest has also rested from his works as God did from his. (Heb. 4:9–10)

Physical rest is important. It's a pattern that's found in creation. But it points us to a greater kind of rest: a spiritual rest that we can only experience in God.

This rest is about enjoying God's blessing and freedom. It's about life the way it was meant to be lived. It's something we can experience now, at least in part. Right now, we can rest in a secure relationship with God because of what Jesus has done for us. God promises that His people will experience this fully one day.

This rest is about "a promised position in which one is rightly related to God and partaking of his blessings."[19]

According to the Bible, we can miss out on this rest if we're not careful. "Let us therefore strive to enter that rest . . ." (Heb. 4:11). Pay attention, the Bible says, and work at entering the rest that God has provided for anyone who wants it.

Ultimately, rest is receiving what Jesus has done for us, and finding our security and identity in God.

Jamin Goggin and Kyle Strobel put it well:

> Rest is not inaction or laziness. It is not merely the default result of having nothing to do. Rest is the foundation for our lives in God. . . .
>
> This is most fully understood only when we can come before the Lord in utter silence, not seeking to justify ourselves, prove ourselves, make excuses for ourselves, or even announce our

presence. In the presence of the Lord, we rest in the intercession of the Son and Spirit. In the presence of the Lord, we draw near based on what the Lord has already done for us. There, before the face of God, we find rest and peace in the work of another. . .

We are free to love others and not use them, because we are no longer the center of our universe, but find ourselves in orbit around Christ.

We are free to rest in God's grace.

We are free to know and be known because God has made himself known to us in Christ.

In this freedom we can finally allow ourselves to be known in prayer, and to know the God of love as he cascades his prayers over us.[20]

True rest is finding our security in being known and loved by God. This amazing gift is available to anyone who wants it through Jesus, who offers to make us holy through His life, death, and resurrection.

WHAT TO DO TODAY

In Habit 1 (Make Time), we looked at growth stages and the idea of beginning where you are.

If you are at the Questioning stage, continue to explore what the Bible says about rest and other topics. Ask what and who the Bible says you need in order to experience God's rest.

If you are in the Believing or Growing stages, lean further into resting well. Consider what Jesus has done for you and the knowledge that you are treasured and profoundly loved by God as you begin your time of rest. Ask God what you can do to enjoy this truth more profoundly today.

Begin where you are, use what time you have, do what you can to rest today. It's one of God's greatest gifts.

Reflect and Respond

REVIEW

Developing a habit of rest is hard work. It requires courage and intentionality.

In this habit, we:

- follow God's example
- receive what Jesus has done for us
- find our security and identity in God
- love others rather than use them because Christ becomes our center

CONSIDER

- Look for leisure activities that bring you closer to God, people, beauty, and make you feel more alive.
- Does taking a full day off seem impossible for you at this point in your life? How might you shrink the challenge? What period of time is doable once a week—a half day, a morning, an afternoon or evening, an hour?
- Start where you are, do what you can.

ACTION

- **Take some time to rest today.**
- **Look ahead and plan a Sabbath day,** an entire day to rest and enjoy God's presence and His gifts.

HABIT #2: REST AND REFRESH

Review

AS WE PRACTICED the habit of rest, we:

- introduced the rhythm of work and rest.
- looked at rest as a command, a promise, and a need.
- discovered that the benefits of rest are profound, but may not cost you anything.
- learned that true rest comes from being wholehearted: living out of our core, and being known and loved.
- reflected on the true rest that comes from knowing that we are known and loved by God through what Jesus has done.

RESOURCES

Visit gospelforlife.com/rest for resources on this habit.

EVALUATION

Think about the habit of rest.

- What went well for you?
- Where did you succeed, even a little bit?
- What can you celebrate?

WHAT TO DO TODAY

1. **Rest.** Take a small amount of time for rest; or make plans for a longer period of time (a day or partial day) for Sabbath rest. If you're not ready for a full day, then shrink the challenge. Do what you can.

2. **Check out some of our recommended resources** on rest, including a helpful video by Bible Project. Visit gospelforlife .com/rest/.

3. **Make a list of activities** that you find replenishing, and that fill your soul with joy.

4. If you're struggling with this habit, **ask God to reveal what is keeping you from the rest He desires for you.** Talk to a friend about why resting is a hard habit to develop.

5. **Then do what you can to make time** for your new habits in the coming week.

Group Discussion Questions

READ HEBREWS 4:1-11.

1. This passage is about the Israelites in the wilderness who didn't enter God's rest (the promised land) because of their disbelief. They heard the good news (Ex. 34:6-7) but missed out on God's promises. What are some ways that we may repeat their mistake?

2. This passage points us to the different dimensions of rest in the Bible. Scripture talks about physical rest in the Sabbath (Ex. 20:8-11). It talks about Jesus providing rest for our souls (Matt. 11:28-30). It talks about our ultimate rest, in which we enter into all of God's promises (Heb. 4:1-11). How does this give us a deeper understanding of what rest is?

3. Sabbath is meant to be a gift, but many of us find it hard to receive this gift. Why do you think we sometimes have a hard time resting?

4. What are some steps you can take to build a weekly rhythm of rest into your life, with one full day free from obligations, dedicated to restoring your soul and enjoying God and others?

5. How can you celebrate your progress in building more rest into your life?

6. What questions do you have about rest?

Engage the Bible

HABIT

Engage the Bible by reading or listening to Scripture daily.

ASPIRATION

To hear God through His Word, and be shaped by what He's revealed.

CHOOSE YOUR ACTIONS

Choose one or more of the following:

- Choose a format that works for you: paper, electronic, or audio.
- Investigate Bible reading plans, and choose one that interests you and fits your schedule.
- Find friends who want to read the Bible regularly, and form a group for discussion and mutual support.

HABIT 3, LESSON 1

Introducing Habit #3:
Engage the Bible

ENGAGING THE BIBLE IS ESSENTIAL to the Christian life.

Welcome to Habit 3.

Starting today, I invite you to begin a new habit: engage the Bible by reading or listening to Scripture every day.

THE IMPORTANCE OF THE BIBLE

Reading or listening to absorb the Bible is crucial for spiritual growth. Donald Whitney, a leading teacher on spiritual disciples, writes, "No Spiritual Discipline is more important than the intake of God's Word. Nothing can substitute for it. There simply is no healthy Christian life apart from a diet of the milk and meat of Scripture."[1]

The late philanthropist and pastor George Müller said something similar: "The vigour of our spiritual life will be in exact proportion to the place held by the Bible in our life and thoughts."[2]

Engaging the Bible is so important that I consider it to be one of three core habits of the Christian life. While all the habits in this book are helpful, these three habits are essential.

A quick note about core habits: This book contains 8 habits. I call 3 of them core habits:

- Engage the Bible
- Speak with God
- Worship and Belong

All of the habits in this book are important. The reality is that *all* the habits are interrelated and also foundational. For example:

- You have to make time (Habit 1) in order to do the core habits.
- You have to care for your body (Habit 6) and rest (Habit 2) in order to optimally engage the core habits.
- You have to rightly prioritize (Habit 7) in order for the core habits (Bible, prayer, church) to be done properly.
- You need to figure out how to maintain these habits over the long haul (Habit 8) to make them stick.

If all the habits are important, why do I call three of them core habits? Because they're the basics that matter most. They're like playing scales in piano, or shooting baskets in basketball. You need other skills besides playing scales or shooting baskets, but you never outgrow these basic practices.

Core habits are super-habits, the fundamentals we must master. "Without the fundamentals, the details are useless. With the fundamentals, tiny gains can add up to something very significant," writes James Clear.[3] Pay attention to all the habits, but really master the core habits.

Although the Bible is important, many have a hard time absorbing it. A study in Canada found that the majority of Christians read the Bible either seldom or never.[4] George Guthrie, professor of New Testament at Regent College, says that if you ask a hundred church members if they read the Bible at least once in the past week, sixty-eight will say no. Even worse, only thirty-seven will say it's made any difference in their lives.[5]

Reading or listening to the Bible may be the most effective and ignored strategy for spiritual growth.

HOW TO START

This habit may seem scary at first. Shrink the challenge, and make it small enough that you're confident you can succeed.

Getting started isn't as hard as you might think.

1. **Choose a format.** If you're an auditory learner, consider listening to the Bible. If you prefer to read, that's great too. We'll dig in to some options tomorrow, but for now, think about how you enjoy learning.

2. **Choose a goal.** Again, be realistic. Listening to the Bible in a year takes around 75 hours, which works out to less than 15 minutes a day over the course of a year. Reading the Bible over two years takes only 7–8 minutes a day. This option is great for people who've never read the Bible before. Another great option is to select one book of the Bible to read and reread for a period of time (one to three months or more), allowing the book to soak deep into your heart.

3. **Practice.** David Mathis says it well: "At the end of the day, there is simply no replacement for finding a regular time and place, blocking out distractions, putting your nose in the text, and letting your mind and heart be led and captured and thrilled by God himself communicating to us in his objective written words."[6]

4. **Don't give up.** Many people quit if they miss a day or two. You can avoid this mistake by using the clean slate policy. No guilt, no shame. Just start where you are, do what you can, and carry on.

HOW LONG DOES IT TAKE TO READ THE BIBLE?[7]

How many days or years would it take for the average person (reading 120 words a minute) to read the Bible if they read this many minutes per day?

	40 DAYS	90 DAYS	1 YEAR	2 YEARS
OLD TESTAMENT	1 hour 39 minutes	44 minutes	11 minutes	5 minutes
NEW TESTAMENT	29 minutes	13 minutes	3 minutes	2 minutes
WHOLE BIBLE	2 hours 7 minutes	57 minutes	14 minutes	7 minutes

MAKE YOUR CHOICE

The number of apps, websites, and paper Bibles is staggering. You can find a list of my favorite recommendations at gospelforlife.com/Bible.

It's important to get going with a good option rather than trying to find the perfect option. Pick a Bible and start reading or listening. Experiment to find what works best for you.

If you don't own a good study Bible yet, then I recommend you make the investment. A good study Bible provides context, explanations, and connections to related passages to help you better understand the passage you are reading.

WHAT TO DO TODAY

If you don't already have a Bible or Bible app, or if your love of reading or listening to the Bible needs a refresh:

- Check out the options listed at gospelforlife.com/Bible.
- Choose one. Give it a try. Experiment. Find what works for you. The most important thing is to start.

If you already have a plan that brings joy and life as you read or listen to the Bible, that's awesome.

Spend a few minutes reading or listening to the Bible today.

Then, keep doing what you can with your previous habits. We'd still like you to:

- **Continue to make time.** Look over your week and make time to practice your habits each day.
- **Rest.** Take a small amount of time each day for an activity that renews you. Work toward taking a full day off each week to pursue activities that bring you closer to God, people, beauty, and meaning.

Reflect and Respond

REVIEW

The Bible is crucial for spiritual growth.

Many Christians don't regularly engage with the Bible. When we don't read or listen to the Bible, we starve our heart, mind, and thoughts of the spiritual nourishment we need most.

CONSIDER

- **Choose your format.** If you haven't already done so, choose an option from the list at gospelforlife.com/Bible.
- **Choose your goal.** Be realistic. Start small. You can find a variety of plans at the link mentioned above.
- **Just get started. Don't worry about doing it perfectly.**
- **Don't give up.** If you miss a day, wipe the slate clean and start fresh.

DISCUSS

1. How do you feel about reading or listening to the Bible every day?
2. What will you do today to read or listen to the Bible?

Tips for Engaging Scripture Effectively

READING AND LISTENING to the Bible isn't easy, but it's not as hard as you think. It's worth the effort.

I'd be lying if I told you that absorbing the Bible is easy. Frankly, there are some parts of the Bible that are hard to understand.

Peter, a key leader in the early church and author of two books in the Bible, also found parts of the Bible hard to understand. He spoke candidly about some of Paul's letters in the Bible: "There are some things in them that are hard to understand" (2 Peter 3:16). We're in good company!

The good news is that we have more resources to help us than at any other time in history. Absorbing the Bible isn't easy, but it's not as hard as you'd think. In fact, it's easier than it's ever been before.

SOME PRACTICAL TIPS

1. **Believe it's worth it.** When you get to the hard parts, remember that they are there for a reason. The Bible says, "All Scrip-

ture is breathed out by God and profitable for teaching, for reproof, for correction, and for training in righteousness, that the man of God may be complete, equipped for every good work" (2 Tim. 3:16–17). Everything in Scripture is good, so lean in.

2. **Follow a plan.** Find a plan that works for you.

3. **Use good tools.** A Bible with study notes is a great help. So are the explainer videos at BibleProject.[8] A good Bible companion or commentary can also come in handy.

4. **Read or listen with others if possible.** Find a reading partner for accountability, encouragement, and discussion.

5. **Pray. Ask for God's help as you read or listen.** David Mathis calls this the X factor in Bible reading: "No matter how thin your training, no matter how spotty your routine, the Helper stands ready. Take up the text in confidence that God is primed to bless your being with his very breath."[9]

6. **Get the big picture.** It's okay if you don't understand every detail. Get a broad understanding or big picture.

7. **Expect to learn something.**

8. **Apply it to your life.** As you read or listen, look for a thought, insight, or action to take into your life. Puritan preacher Thomas Watson said, "Take every word as spoken to yourselves. When the word thunders against sin, think thus: 'God means my sins;' when it presseth any duty, 'God intends me in this.' Many put off scripture from themselves, as if it only concerned those who lived in the time when it was written; but if you intend to profit by the word, bring it home to yourselves: a medicine will do no good, unless it be applied."[10]

If you haven't already done so, check out the updated list of tools at gospelforlife.com/Bible.

START SLOW

I love this advice from Welsh pastor Geoffrey Thomas:

> Do not expect to master the Bible in a day, or a month, or a year. Rather expect often to be puzzled by its contents. It is not all equally clear. Great men of God often feel like absolute novices when they read the Word. . . . So do not expect always to get an emotional charge or a feeling of quiet peace when you read the Bible. . . .
>
> Let the Word break over your heart and mind again and again as the years go by, and imperceptibly there will come great changes in your attitude and outlook and conduct.[11]

It may take time, but God's Word has the power to change your life.

WHAT TO DO TODAY

Spend a few minutes reading or listening to the Bible.

Keep up the good work with your first two habits. Remember to keep it small enough that it is doable. Make time for a restful or relaxing activity and plan your next session to work through this book.

Reflect and Respond

SUMMARY

Tips for reading or listening to the Bible:

- Believe it's worth it.
- Follow a plan.
- Use good tools, like a good study Bible or commentary.
- Read or listen with others if possible. Find a reading partner for accountability, encouragement, and discussion.
- Pray. Ask for God's help as you read or listen.
- Get the big picture. Videos at BibleProject are excellent for this.
- Expect to learn something.
- Apply it to your life.

CONSIDER

- Some parts of the Bible are hard to understand. Expect to have questions. Ask God to provide you with more understanding. Use good Bible study tools and ask others (e.g., mentors, teachers, pastors) for help.
- "Do not expect always to get an emotional charge or a feeling of quiet peace when you read the Bible."[12]
- Believe it's worth it. Feast on the Bible. It's the very best of food for our heart, mind, and soul.

DISCUSS

1. What do you find difficult about reading or listening to the Bible?
2. What small steps will you take to read or listen to the Bible today?

The Storyline of the Bible

ONE OF THE BIGGEST KEYS to absorbing the Bible is to understand how the story fits together.

There's no question. Reading the Bible can get complicated. The Bible is a huge book written by many authors over hundreds of years, and includes history, poetry, and some other kinds of writing that are uncommon today.

It's easy to overcomplicate things and get lost, or even give up.

If we want to build a sustainable habit of reading or listening to the Bible, we need to get some tools to help keep things simple.

UNDERSTAND THE STORY

Every story has a plot. Usually, things begin well. We meet a character who wants something. Before long, the character faces an obstacle. The obstacle makes it difficult for the character to get what they want, and things get worse. Finally, there's a breakthrough, and everything changes.

Almost every story follows this structure. The Bible is no exception. In the Bible, God is the main character. This may come as a surprise. We tend to think that people like Abraham, Moses, David, Peter, John, and Paul are the main characters. People have an important role in the story, but God has the starring role.

When the story starts, things are going well. God creates the world and everything in it. God creates humans in His own image; He is present with us and passionate about His relationship with us.

But then things go horribly wrong. Humanity rebels against God, and the world becomes a mess. God soon initiates a plan to reestablish His presence with us, but at first, things don't seem to work out. For hundreds of years, things keep getting worse until it looks like all hope is lost.

Then, God sends His Son Jesus. He becomes human and dwells with us. Even better, He pays the price for our rebellion against God, allowing us to reenter a relationship with God based on His perfect record. Jesus promises to come back again and set the world right.

In the meantime, God dwells with His people again through the Holy Spirit. The world is still a mess, but God is now with us in the middle of the mess. We look forward to the day that God will re-create the earth. In the meantime, we get to enjoy His presence and tell others about this story.

That's it. That's the storyline of the Bible.

FIND YOUR PLACE

When you're reading or listening to the Bible, it's important to understand where you are in the story.

- If you're in Genesis 1–2, you're in the beginning of the story. You're meeting the main character, God, and the supporting characters, us.
- If you're in Genesis 3–11, you're learning about how things went so wrong. These first two sections are critical to understanding why the world is beautiful and yet broken.
- If you're in any other part of the Old Testament, you're in the part where God begins to reestablish a relationship with us. This part has some highlights, but things also get pretty bleak sometimes. Things don't seem to be working out.
- If you're in the Gospels in the New Testament, you're at the climax of the story. God firmly reestablishes His presence with us by sending Jesus, and Jesus does all that's necessary to restore our relationship with God and to conquer evil.
- If you're in the rest of the New Testament (Acts through Revelation), you're between the climax and the ending. God is present with His people again, but the world is still a mess until Jesus comes back again, and God re-creates the world.

One of the biggest keys to absorbing the Bible is to understand where we are in the story. It will help us understand how each part fits within the bigger story.

We also need to realize that we're part of the story that the Bible describes. We live in the last part of the story between the climax and the ending. The Bible isn't just a story; it's our story.

WHAT TO DO TODAY

1. **Make time to read or listen to the Bible.**
2. **Keep up your success so far** by making time each day to rest, read or listen to Scripture, and read these lessons.

Reflect and Respond

REVIEW

Understanding the storyline of the Bible helps us to avoid getting lost so we can keep going with the habit of reading or listening to the Bible.

In the Bible, God is the main character.

The Bible's Story:

1. **Beginning** (Genesis 1–2)—God creates the world, and it is good. Humanity enjoys intimacy with God.
2. **Crisis** (Genesis 3–11)—Humanity rebels against God's rule. Sin damages everything, including our relationship with God.
3. **God begins His rescue plan** (Genesis 12–Malachi)—God initiates His rescue plan to reestablish His relationship with people and fix this broken world. We see glimmers of hope, but people keep rebelling against God.
4. **Climax** (Matthew–John)—God reestablishes His presence with us through the life, death, and resurrection of Jesus.
5. **Waiting** (Acts–Revelation)—The good news of Jesus' reign spreads throughout the world. We get to enjoy new life and announce this good news to others while we wait for Jesus to return and re-create heaven and earth.

We live in the waiting period. We enjoy relationship with God and tell others His story. It's our story too.

CONSIDER

- Do you read or listen to the Bible to understand your life or to learn about God, His thoughts, His ways, and what He desires? How does this change your perspective?
- Place yourself in the Bible's story. How does your story fit in the larger story of the Bible, the story of what God is doing in this world?

DISCUSS

1. What part of the Bible do you enjoy the most?
2. What part of the Bible's story are you least comfortable with?
3. How can you keep things simple as you read or listen to the Bible today?

HABIT 3, LESSON 4

Asking the Right Questions

WHEN YOU READ OR LISTEN to the Bible, ask the right questions.

In the last lesson we focused on understanding the story of the Bible. In this lesson we will add a few more tools to help us keep things simple and engaging.

THE RIGHT QUESTIONS

When it comes to absorbing the Bible, the right question makes all the difference.

Here are some questions that you may find helpful.

1. **Where am I in the Bible's story?** Am I in the beginning (Genesis 1–2), the crisis (Genesis 3–11), the quest to set things right (Genesis 12–Malachi), the climax (God reestablishes His presence, Matthew–John), or waiting for resolution (Acts–Revelation)?

2. **What genre (form of literature) is it?** The Bible contains many different kinds of literature, and each one requires a different approach. There's narrative (Genesis–Esther and Matthew–Acts), poetry and wisdom literature (Job–Song of Solomon), prophetic literature (Isaiah–Malachi), and letters (Romans–Revelation). Within these main categories, there are also other kinds of literature, like parables (stories that teach a lesson) and apocalyptic literature (surreal, symbolic literature that shows us the spiritual realm). You don't need an advanced knowledge of genres, but you do need a basic understanding of what kind of literature you're reading so you can understand what's being communicated.

3. **What do you learn about God?** As the main character of the Bible, aspects of God are revealed in every passage. Does the passage reveal God as Creator, Judge, Father, Redeemer, or some other image? Does the passage reveal one or more of God's qualities, that He is infinite, eternal, unchanging, all-powerful, all-knowing, present everywhere, wise, faithful, good, just, merciful, gracious, loving, holy, or glorious?

4. **What do you learn about people?** Who are the people in the passage, and how are we like them? The Bible often reveals a human need, and shows how that need can be met in God. Usually, it shows us a need that Jesus met by becoming human, making us right with God, and beginning to set everything right again.

5. **How does this Scripture reshape the way I see the world?** Scripture reveals the world the way it really is. We read Scripture so that we begin to rethink our primary story, the way we see and explain the world. As you read the Bible, ask God to change the way you see the world around you, including

history, your relationships, culture, and the unseen world. Get caught up in the larger story of what God is doing in the world.

These questions are great for someone who's just started absorbing the Bible, and they're also good for experts. You'll never outgrow these questions.

LOOK FOR THEMES

As you read, keep your eye out for various themes. Here are a couple you can try.

Tim Kerr, a pastor in Toronto, marks his Bible with colors according to these themes:

- blue—the character of God (who He is, what He is like)
- green—promises of God
- orange—prayers of Scripture
- red—redemptive
- yellow—anything else

Steve Mathewson, a pastor near Chicago, suggests a similar approach:

- red—God's salvation
- purple—God's King/Kingdom
- blue—God's presence
- yellow—God's power
- green—God's kindness (grace, mercy)
- orange—God's judgment[13]

Even if you don't highlight your Bible like this, keep an eye out for these themes.

TYING THINGS TOGETHER

Does this sound complicated? For now, start where you are and pick a tool to keep things simple and engaging. We're meant to read the Bible repeatedly for the rest of our lives. We want to become a Psalm 1 kind of person: "his delight is in the law of the LORD, and on his law he meditates day and night" (Ps. 1:2). We have a lifetime to keep going deeper.

Absorbing Scripture can seem hard at first, but having our desires, thoughts, and behaviors aligned with God is worth the effort. Keep at it!

Reflect and Respond

SUMMARY

Keep engaging the Bible every day. Find a plan and format that works for you, ask for God's help, and make it a regular part of your daily routine. Don't get discouraged if you find it hard. Ask for help from others. Just keep going. It's worth it!

As you read, understanding the story of the Bible and asking the right questions will help to keep the Bible understandable and engaging. Start by asking:

1. Where am I in the story (beginning, crisis, quest, climax, waiting for resolution)?
2. What genre (form of literature) is it?
3. What do I learn about God?
4. What do I learn about people?
5. How does this Scripture reshape the way I see the world?

Look for recurring themes in Scripture, such as God's character, promises, kingdom, etc.

CONSIDER

How is it going with engaging the Bible?

Remember, the way to succeed at a new habit is to start by making it small, and to tie the new habit to something that happens already. If you're struggling, make the habit smaller. Try reading or listening for a shorter time each day, or experiment with a different trigger. For example, read the Bible when you wake up, or listen to the Bible as you get ready for the day or commute. Keep experimenting and find what works for you.

DISCUSS

1. What tool will you use and what questions will you ask as you read or listen to the Bible today?
2. What small steps will you take to read or listen to the Bible today?

HABIT 3, LESSON 5

It's All About Jesus

WHEN WE ABSORB THE BIBLE, we discover that it's all about Jesus.

The Bible is a collection of sixty-six books, written over 1,500 years by dozens of people. Yet it's one story, with God as the primary author, tying it all together.

The Bible has one central theme: God pursuing a relationship with His people.

It has one central figure: Jesus. He is the central figure of all of history, and He stands at the climax of the whole Bible. Jesus Himself said that the whole Bible points to Him:

"You study the Scriptures diligently because you think that in them you have eternal life. These are the very Scriptures that testify about me." (John 5:39 NIV)

And beginning with Moses and all the Prophets, he interpreted to them in all the Scriptures the things concerning himself. (Luke 24:27)

When we read or listen to the Bible, we should always look for Jesus. The Bible is written to lead us to Him, and to help us get to know Him better.

HOW TO FIND JESUS IN THE BIBLE

How do we find Jesus in the Bible? Here are some tips for what you should watch out for so that you don't miss the One it all points to:

1. **Look for where Jesus is mentioned.** In the New Testament (Matthew to Revelation), this shouldn't be hard. Jesus is on almost every page.
2. **Look for where Jesus is predicted.** There are hundreds of prophecies of Jesus in the Old Testament (Genesis–Malachi). Keep your eye out for these predictions.
3. **Look for where Jesus is anticipated.** For instance, Jesus is prophet, priest, and king. This means that every Hebrew prophet is a signpost to the ultimate Prophet; every king in the Old Testament helps us anticipate and long for the ultimate King; every Old Testament sacrifice helps us anticipate Jesus, who is both the Great High Priest and sacrifice at the same time.
4. **Look for your place in the storyline.** No matter where you are in the Bible, the passage is connected to a plot that centers on Jesus. Always connect the individual stories to the overall storyline.

If you want a great resource that will help, I highly recommend *The Jesus Storybook Bible.*[14] It's a great children's book that deserves to be read by adults too.

Finding Jesus in the Bible is something a beginner can do, but it's also something that the most advanced Bible scholar will still be learning after years of study.

For now, keep an eye out for Jesus when you read or listen to the Bible. Ultimately, the whole story is about Him.

Reflect and Respond

REVIEW

The Bible's collection of writings:

- spans 1,500 years
- is made up of 66 books
- has one primary author (God), with many writers
- has one overarching theme: God's reign and pursuit of a relationship with His people
- has one central figure: Jesus

HOW TO FIND JESUS IN THE BIBLE:

1. **Look for where Jesus is mentioned** in the New Testament.
2. **Look for where Jesus is predicted** in the Old Testament (Genesis–Malachi).
3. **Look for where Jesus is anticipated** as Prophet, Priest (or sacrifice), and King.
4. **Look how the passage connects to the storyline.** Understand each passage in light of the storyline that centers on Jesus.

CONSIDER

Consider reading *The Jesus Storybook Bible* with a child, family, friends, or by yourself. Rediscover the wonder, joy, and faith of Jesus like a child.

DISCUSS

1. What have you encountered in the Bible recently that points to Jesus?
2. What's been the most enjoyable part of reading or listening to the Bible this week?
3. What's been the hardest part of reading or listening to the Bible this week?

HABIT #3: ENGAGE THE BIBLE

Review

Here's a look back at where we've walked together.

- This new habit—engaging the Bible—is essential to the Christian life. It's one of the three core habits that are most important.
- We can get started by following some practical tips:
  - Believe it's worth it.
  - Find a plan that works for you, and follow it.
  - Use good tools, like a study Bible, explainer videos, and commentaries.
  - Read or listen with others if possible.
  - Ask for God's help.
  - Understand the storyline of the Bible.
  - Ask key questions.
  - Look for key themes.
  - Look for Jesus in every part of Scripture.
  - Keep going, even when it feels hard.

RESOURCES

Visit gospelforlife.com/Bible for resources on this habit.

EVALUATION

Think about this habit.

- What went well for you?
- Where did you succeed, even a little bit?
- What can you celebrate?

WHAT TO DO TODAY

1. Engage the Bible by reading or listening to God's Word, praying that God would prepare your heart and reveal His truth to you.
2. Then do what you can with your habits of resting and making time.
3. Set aside fifteen minutes for rest, or make plans for a longer period of time (a day or partial day) for Sabbath rest.
4. Look at your plans for the coming week and make time for these habits, and for continuing to work through this book.

How to Engage the Bible

PLOT	BOOKS
Beginning God creates the world and dwells with us.	**Genesis 1–2** narrative
Crisis How things went wrong.	**Genesis 3–11** narrative
God Begins His Rescue Plan God begins to reestablish a relationship with us; things didn't always go well.	**Genesis–Esther** narrative **Job–Song of Solomon** wisdom & poetry **Isaiah–Malachi** prophecy
Climax Jesus becomes human, restores us to God, and conquers evil.	**Matthew–John** narrative
Waiting Although the world is a mess, God dwells with His people. Jesus will return.	**Acts** narrative **Romans–Revelation** letters

TIPS FOR STUDYING

1. Believe that it's worth it!
2. Follow a plan.
3. Use good tools.
4. Read or listen to the Bible with others.

5. Pray!
6. Get the big picture.
7. Expect to learn something.
8. Apply it to your life.

KEY QUESTIONS

1. Where am I in the story?
2. What genre is it?
3. What can I learn about it?
4. What can I learn about humanity?

TAKEAWAYS

- What stands out?
- What's clear?
- What can I apply?
- Where do I see Jesus?

Group Discussion Questions

READ PSALM 1.

1. The psalmist speaks of delighting in God's law and meditating on it day and night (Ps. 1:2). How is this different from how we normally think about engaging with the Bible?

2. Meditating on God's Word day and night means that we think about how it applies to every part of our lives. What are some practical ways we can do this?

3. The psalmist describes the results of a life that's built on God's law (Ps. 1:3). Jeremiah uses a similar image in Jeremiah 17:7–8. How does God's Word help us to flourish?

4. Many Christians struggle to engage with the Bible consistently. Why do you think this is? What struggles have you experienced in reading or listening to the Bible?

5. What parts of the Bible do you find easiest to read? Which parts do you find hardest?

6. What are some approaches to reading or listening to the Bible that you've found effective?

7. What questions do you have about reading or listening to the Bible?

Speak
with God

HABIT

Speak with God every day through prayer.

ASPIRATION

To live in relationship with God, talking to Him about everything that is going on in your life.

CHOOSE YOUR ACTIONS

Choose one or more of the following:

- Choose a time each day to pray, and set a timer for five minutes.
- Go for a prayer walk. While walking, spend time praying to God and telling Him what is on your mind.
- Keep a prayer journal. Buy a paper journal or use a journaling app, and write your prayers to God.

Introducing Habit #4:
Speak with God

BEGIN TO SPEAK WITH GOD in prayer for at least a few minutes every day.

Welcome to a new habit!

We're going to begin working on a new habit that many find difficult, even though it's a gift from God. Begin to pray every day to God. It's the second of three core habits. While all the habits in this book are important, the three core habits (**Engage the Bible, Speak with God,** and **Worship and Belong**) matter most.

PRAYER IS EASY

In some ways, prayer is both easy and hard at the same time.

On the one hand, prayer is surprisingly easy. You don't have to learn how to pray. There's no formula or procedure. You can just begin to talk with God and share what is on your mind.

In prayer, we can be real, honest, and vulnerable before God.

We're allowed to approach God with whatever is on our minds, and to simply enjoy His presence.

In prayer, we get God's ear. God, who made us and who knows everything about us, invites us to come boldly into His presence and relate to Him. If you don't feel like praying, then pray about that. If you are angry, tempted, or discouraged, then tell God. When we pray, we can tell God whatever is on our mind.

Sometimes we don't know what to say. The Bible teaches us that the Holy Spirit is able to translate our prayers. "In the same way, the Spirit helps us in our weakness. We do not know what we ought to pray for, but the Spirit himself intercedes for us through wordless groans" (Rom. 8:26 NIV). When we don't know what to pray for, the Holy Spirit brings a prayer before God that perfectly matches what we need.

God wants to hear from us. He invites us to come before Him, to tell Him what's on our minds, and to enjoy His presence.

We can learn to pray better, but you already know how to pray. Simply tell God what's on your mind.

PRAYER IS HARD

Although prayer is easy, it's also very hard. It may be one of the hardest things in the world. Our minds wander. We struggle to be honest. We see prayer as a duty, rather than as a privilege. We begin to question whether prayer is worth it.

In his book *A Praying Life*, Paul Miller describes a camping trip in which his daughter Ashley lost a contact lens. "Don't move," he said. "Let's pray."

Ashley burst into tears. "What good does it do? I've prayed for Kim to speak, and she isn't speaking." Kim, Miller's autistic daughter, is mute despite years of speech therapy.

Miller says:

> Few of us have Ashley's courage to articulate the quiet cynicism or spiritual weariness that develops in us when heartfelt prayer goes unanswered. We keep our doubts hidden even from ourselves because we don't want to sound like bad Christians. No reason to add shame to our cynicism. So our hearts shut down.[1]

Prayer is supposed to be easy, but we often find it hard. We begin to worry. We don't know what to say. We have a hard time slowing down. Nobody responds, and it feels like we're talking to ourselves. We wonder if God is there, or if prayer makes a difference.

Prayer is both easy and hard at the same time.

JUST START

"The hardest thing about prayer is the small gap between thinking about praying and actually praying," writes Tim Kerr, "that is, JUST TO BEGIN."[2] The hardest part is to just start praying.

Shrink that gap. Acknowledge any fear, resistance, or discomfort you may feel, and then **take a moment right now to practice your new habit of prayer.** Don't worry about what to say. Recognize that you're in God's presence, talk to Him like anyone else, and tell Him whatever is on your mind. If you find it hard to pray, tell Him that, and ask for His help.

If you're not used to praying, Linette Martin's advice is helpful:

> The way to begin is slowly: I advise five minutes. That may feel impossibly short, but it is better to get a short time established than to begin with a longer one that you give up later as being impractical. It should not be longer on one day because it feels nice and shorter on another day as the mood takes you. Even

if you feel great enthusiasm and want to go on longer one day, please restrict yourself to only five minutes. Set aside the same small block of time day after day after day. It can be done.[3]

We'll be exploring prayer over the next few lessons. Today, just begin. Start where you are: one thought, one sentence, one minute, or more. God loves hearing from us, and He welcomes us into His presence when we pray.

Then do what you can to practice your previous habits:

- **Engage the Bible**.
- **Rest and Refresh**. Take some time to rest every day, and plan a day (or part of a day) of rest this week.
- **Make Time**. If you're reading this, you're already doing it! Well done.

Reflect and Respond

SUMMARY

Prayer Is Easy

- There's no formula or procedure needed. Prayer is just talking with God.
- God invites us to come, to enjoy His presence, and tell Him what's on our minds. He holds a safe space for us, just as we are: for all of our real feelings, messy emotions, wandering thoughts, questions, and doubts.
- When we pray and feel like we don't know what to pray for, the Holy Spirit brings a prayer before God that perfectly matches what we need.

Prayer Is Hard

- Prayer is supposed to be easy, but we often find it hard to do.

- We struggle to be honest.
- It feels like a duty, rather than a privilege.
- We have a hard time slowing down, our thoughts wander, or we don't know what to say.
- We wonder if God is there, or if prayer makes a difference.

Just Start

- Reduce the challenge. Don't get overwhelmed.
- Tell God if you feel resistant or uncomfortable.
- Start where you are.

CONSIDER

- How do you feel about talking to God every day? Does it feel like a gift or an obligation?
- Can you think of a time that prayer came easily to you?

DISCUSS

1. When and where is prayer easy for you?
2. What do you find hard about prayer?
3. What small step will you take to grow a little more in prayer today?
4. What can you pray about right now?

HABIT 4, LESSON 2

Pray Like a Child

TO LEARN HOW TO PRAY, become like a child.

On a number of occasions, Jesus gave some strange advice to His followers. He told them to become like children.

Here's one example:

> Truly, I say to you, unless you turn and become like children, you will never enter the kingdom of heaven. Whoever humbles himself like this child is the greatest in the kingdom of heaven. (Matt. 18:3–4)

When Jesus said these words, children weren't valued highly. They were the most powerless members of society. They were loved by their families but had no power, status, or privilege apart from that love. Few of us want to adopt an attitude of humility and powerlessness. Jesus' words would have been surprising.

They're no less surprising today. We like to pretend that we're mature and that we don't need help. Jesus says that the way to approach God is to flip this. To learn how to pray, become like a child.

LEARNING TO BE MESSY

Children are messy. They don't wait until they are presentable before they reach out to parents for help. Frankly, children can be a little self-absorbed. They don't worry about whether their request is convenient or selfish. They come just as they are.

Parents sometimes get frustrated, especially in the middle of the night. Overall, though, parents love hearing from their children, even if what they say is immature or hard to understand. They love to hear their children babble. They welcome their children, even when they're messy.

In the same way, God loves it when we come to Him, even when we're messy. God loves when we come to Him needy and honest.

LEARNING TO BE NEEDY

We don't like to be needy. Children, on the other hand, don't seem to struggle with being dependent on their parents.

When we stop being dependent, we stop praying. One of the keys to prayer is to become like a little child in our relationship with God and to understand that we never stop needing Him to provide for us.

God isn't put off by our neediness. He invites us to recognize that we're needy, and then to turn to Him in confidence.

LEARNING TO TRUST

Children are meant to grow up in a secure environment. It's important for children to develop secure attachments, and to know that they are loved no matter what they do.

Even if we experience that security as children, we eventually grow older and discover that our parents aren't as powerful or as perfect as we hoped.

God, however, is all-powerful, and His love never wavers. He invites us to rest in the security of His love and in the knowledge that He is all-powerful.

When you pray, remember that you are praying to your Father. He loves hearing from His children, and only He is powerful enough to meet our needs. Jesus told us to come and ask, seek, and knock, believing that God is good, and that He loves giving good gifts to His children (Matt. 7:7–11).

I love how Jared Wilson puts it:

> Look, prayer is spilling your guts. It doesn't have to be pretty. It doesn't have to be tidy. It doesn't have to be particularly eloquent or even particularly intelligent. But the Bible is how God speaks to us and prayer is how we speak to God. These two rhythms form the dynamic of our friendship with the God of the universe.[4]

YOUR ASSIGNMENT

As you pray today, don't try to make yourself presentable to God. Come as a child. Bring your messiness and neediness to God. Remind yourself that He cares for you and that He loves to hear from you. He welcomes us, and He's powerful enough to meet our needs.

Today, speak with God in heartfelt prayer. Tell God what's on your mind. He loves when we speak to Him in prayer.

Reflect and Respond

SUMMARY

To pray like a child means:

- adopting an attitude of humility and dependence
- being okay with coming to God honestly with our needs
- learning to trust that only God is powerful enough to provide and that He desires to give good gifts to His children

CONSIDER

When you come to God, are you more . . .

- free to be messy or "holding it all together" perfectly?
- needy or needing to be in control?
- trusting in God's provision or anxious for the outcome you desire?

DISCUSS

1. What makes it hard for you to pray like a child?
2. What small steps can you take today to pray like a child?

HABIT 4, LESSON 3

Learning Prayer

WHEN IT COMES TO PRAYER, we're all beginners.

A publisher asked a well-known pastor and author to write a book on prayer. In a moment of honesty, he replied that the writer of such a book would have to be older, more seasoned, and more prayerful than he was. He suggested some other names. The publisher smiled. He had asked those authors too, and they said the same thing. "Who can write or speak at any length easily on the mystery of prayer?" he asked.[5]

If it feels like you're a beginner in praying, be encouraged. We're all there.

Thankfully, Jesus gave some advice to beginners like us on how to pray.

HOW TO PRAY

Jesus emphasized praying honestly and simply, rather than putting on a performance:

"And when you pray, you must not be like the hypocrites. For they love to stand and pray in the synagogues and at the street corners, that they may be seen by others. Truly, I say to you, they have received their reward. But when you pray, go into your room and shut the door and pray to your Father who is in secret. And your Father who sees in secret will reward you.

"And when you pray, do not heap up empty phrases as the Gentiles do, for they think that they will be heard for their many words. Do not be like them, for your Father knows what you need before you ask him." (Matt. 6:5–8)

Don't pray to impress anyone. Remember that God is eager to meet with you. God isn't impressed with our attempts to impress Him either. He simply wants us to come and tell Him, plainly and without pretense, what we need. He is our Father, and He loves to hear from us.

Refuse to play religious games with your prayer. Just come simply, knowing that God welcomes you.

WHAT TO PRAY

Jesus gives us a model prayer that we can use to shape our own prayers.

"Pray then like this:

"Our Father in heaven,
hallowed be your name.
Your kingdom come,
your will be done,
on earth as it is in heaven.

Give us this day our daily bread,
and forgive us our debts,
as we also have forgiven our debtors.
And lead us not into temptation,
but deliver us from evil." (Matt. 6:9–13)

Based on Jesus' prayer, here are some things we can include in our prayers:

- Thank God that He is our Father and that He cares for us. There is nothing we can do to get God to love us more or less than He already does. He welcomes us.
- Worship God for who He is. He is holy and glorious, and He deserves our praise.
- Acknowledge His ownership of your life and the entire universe. Ask for more of God's reign in your life and the world around you.
- Bring your needs and troubles to God. Confess your anxieties, and ask Him to give you a heart that trusts Him to meet your needs.
- Ask God to forgive you and to help you overcome temptation.

Jesus didn't give this prayer as a formula. He gave it as a pattern we can follow to shape our own prayers, knowing that we often learn best from a good example.

TODAY

God welcomes you to come and pray, honestly and without pretense. Jesus even offers us a template for prayer that allows us to speak to God about the details of our lives.

God loves when we come to Him as our Father. He can't wait to hear from you today.

Reflect and Respond

SUMMARY

We are all beginners, able to learn and grow in prayer. Jesus tells us:

How to Pray

- honestly and simply
- in secret
- without trying to impress others

What to Pray

- Give thanks that God is our loving Father.
- Worship God for who He is.
- Acknowledge God's ownership of all things, and ask for more of His reign in your life and in the world around you.
- Bring your needs and troubles to God.
- Ask God to forgive you and help you overcome temptation.

CONSIDER

- When are you tempted to try impressing people with your prayers?
- Do you ever feel like prayer is just another duty or obligation?
- How could you make your prayers more simple and honest?

DISCUSS

1. How can you keep prayer from becoming a religious performance in your life?
2. What are some things that you can pray about today?

HABIT 4, LESSON 4

Manage Life Through Prayer

THINK OF PRAYER as how you manage your life, not as something you add to your life.

If you haven't already noticed, I really like Paul Miller's book *A Praying Life*. I read it a few years ago, and found it honest and encouraging. Few books have helped me pray as much as this book did.

Miller is a regular guy. He has a job, plus he's a husband and father. One of his children has some significant health issues.

In the book, Miller describes a time that he felt frustrated with his daughter's behavior. He tried to solve the problem himself, but it didn't work. He consulted a neurologist, who prescribed a drug, but that didn't work. Finally, he prayed about it, and the problem went away.

Gradually, as he prayed for his children, he began to see God work in their lives. He realized that he did his best parenting through prayer. He began to speak less to the kids and more to God. He writes:

Prayer is where I do my best work as a husband, dad, worker, and friend. I'm aware of the weeds of unbelief in me and the struggles in others' lives. The Holy Spirit puts his finger on issues that only he can solve. I'm actually managing my life through my daily prayer time. I'm shaping my heart, my work, my family—in fact, everything that is dear to me—through prayer in fellowship with my heavenly Father. I'm doing that because I don't have control over my heart and life or the hearts and lives of those around me. But God does.[7]

PRAYER IS NOT JUST ANOTHER THING

By this point in the book, you may feel that you've been given a lot to do. You may be struggling with finding energy and motivation to practice these habits. Even though the habits are small, it's sometimes hard to add anything new to our lives.

Today, I'd like to encourage you to see prayer not as something you're adding, but as a way to manage some of the stress and complexity in your life. Don't see it as another thing. See it as a way to shift some of your stress to God.

The Bible tells us:

Humble yourselves, therefore, under the mighty hand of God so that at the proper time he may exalt you, casting all your anxieties on him, because he cares for you.
(1 Peter 5:6–7)

Casting our anxieties on God is a good thing. Don't try to carry them—even the small ones—yourself. He is big enough to handle whatever is on your mind. Besides, He cares for you. How great is that?

Peter tells us that if we don't give our anxieties to God, it's a form of pride. It shows that we think we can handle our lives without God's help. It's far better to admit the truth. We all need God's help. The good news? He's willing to give us that help.

WHAT'S ON YOUR MIND?

Today, I'd like to ask you to try an experiment.

Step 1: List five things you're stressed, worried, or thinking about. Write or draw them to get them off your mind.

Step 2: Give these things to God. Pray about them. Cast your anxieties on Him.

Step 3: If you catch yourself stressed or worrying about them later, gently give yourself permission to give them back to God.

Experiment with managing your daily life through prayer.

Reflect and Respond

REVIEW

- Prayer is not just another thing to do or habit to integrate.
- Prayer is a way to manage the stress and complexity in life.
- In prayer we shift our anxieties and concerns to God's care.
- Through prayer we grow in humility as we let go of pride in our own abilities.
- We need God's help in all things.
- God cares for us and delights in giving us the help we need.

CONSIDER

Recall today's experiment of praying for five things that you're stressed, worried, or thinking about.

1. Did you become anxious or stressed about these things later in the day?
2. Were you able to pause and bring your stress or worry back to God in prayer?
3. Was it easy or difficult to give your anxiety and stress back to God?

DISCUSS

1. When do you feel like something is "too small" for you to speak with God about it?
2. What are some anxieties that you want to hand over to God today?

Prayer Tools

TRY JOURNALING PRAYERS, and develop a simple plan to pray for the significant people and things in your life.

When it comes to prayer, it's best to keep things simple. Pray regularly and tell God whatever is on your mind. Try praying Scripture, like the Psalms or the prayer that Jesus taught us. Begin simply, and pray regularly. God loves to hear from you!

If that's all you need, then keep it that simple.

If you're ready for more of a challenge or want more structure, I'd encourage you to try a couple of approaches to praying. One is to write our prayers; the other is to keep track of people and things we want to pray for.

PRAYER JOURNALS

One pastor found that his mind wandered when he prayed. He bought simple spiral-bound notebooks and recorded what happened the previous day, what he learned, and what he thought God was teaching him. He included prayers if he felt like it. Later on, he moved to recording his prayers on a computer. Decades later, his journals record the faithfulness of God, the highs and lows of life, stories of his family and friends, and more.

Some find that writing prayers helps to slow them down. It makes it easier to stay focused. It forces specificity.

If you enjoy writing, then try journaling your prayers. It doesn't work for everyone, but some have found it to be very helpful.

A SIMPLE PLAN FOR PRAYER

There are lots of things to pray for, but we lose track of many of them or get overwhelmed. I've found that a simple plan for praying helps.

Here are a few options for developing a simple plan:

- Pray for different things on different days of the week. For instance, pray for family on Monday and Thursday, friends on Tuesday and Friday, and ministries on Wednesday and Saturday.
- Write prayer requests on recipe cards under different categories (family, friends, ministry, personal requests, etc.). Every day, pray for one or two cards in each category.
- Try the free PrayerMate app,[8] which helps you pray for the people and causes that you care about.
- Record your requests and answers to prayer and review them when you need encouragement.

LEARN HOW YOU PRAY BEST

Scripture encourages us to "pray without ceasing" (1 Thess. 5:17). Ideally, this means that we set aside specific times to pray, and then continue to speak to God throughout the day about everything that happens.

Some people find it better to set extended time aside for prayer in the morning. Some prefer the evening. Some sprinkle prayer throughout the day at specific times. God invites us to speak to Him, and we're free to figure out how to make this work in our individual lives.

Some like to journal and plan prayers; some don't. Experiment, and find the practices that help you cultivate a rich prayer life.

Keep experimenting. Find what works for you, and just keep praying.

Reflect and Respond

REVIEW

Aim to keep your prayers:

- simple
- regular
- honest (tell God whatever's on your mind)

It's helpful to base our prayers on Scriptures like the Psalms and the Lord's Prayer, but that isn't a prerequisite or necessity. We can come to God and tell Him what's on our minds.

Experiment with prayer practices and tools to:

- keep your heart and mind connected with God
- keep track of people and things you want to pray for
- keep track of God's provisions and answers

CONSIDER

If you want to refresh your prayer habit, try adding a new practice to your prayer time. Remember: start small, shrink the practice, then shrink it again if necessary. Make sure it's small enough that you can do it regularly.

Here are a few ideas to try:

- Journal your prayers.
- Compose songs or drawings of your prayer.
- Listen to instrumental music while you pray.
- Pray together with a friend or family member.
- Pray in a different physical posture or while active: kneeling, face down, lying down, standing, running, working out, walking the dog, doing household chores, gardening, or doing yard work.
- Create a simple prayer plan using a list, recipe cards, spreadsheet, or the PrayerMate app.
- Add the words of a written prayer (from Scripture, or from a book like *Every Moment Holy*[9] or *The Valley of Vision*[10]) to your daily or weekly prayers.

Ready for a more advanced challenge? Try a daily prayer rhythm. For example:

- morning and evening
- before or after breakfast, lunch, and dinner
- 6 a.m., 9 a.m., noon, 3 p.m., and 6 p.m.

DISCUSS

1. What have you learned (so far) about what you need to pray well (time of day, tools, planned/unplanned, etc.)?
2. What prayer practice, tool(s), or plan will you use to help you pray today?
3. What are some things you want to hand over to God today?

HABIT #4:
SPEAK WITH GOD

Review

SO FAR WE'VE COVERED a number of habits, including two of the core habits that are essential to the Christian life:

- Engage the Bible
- Speak with God

Here's what we learned about the habit of praying for at least a few minutes every day to God.

- Prayer is both easy and hard.
- It's okay to be messy and needy in our prayers.
- Jesus gave us a pattern for prayer (Matt. 6:9–13).
- Prayer is a way to manage life, rather than something to add to our lives.
- Journals and tools can help us to pray.

Remember to keep things simple. God loves when we come to Him in prayer.

RESOURCES

Visit gospelforlife.com/pray for resources on this habit.

EVALUATION

Think about this habit.

- What went well for you?
- Where did you succeed, even a little bit?
- What can you celebrate?

WHAT TO DO TODAY

1. Pray.
2. Then do what you can to practice your other habits:
   - Read or listen to the Bible.
   - Take a small amount of time for rest; make plans for a longer period of time (a day or partial day) for Sabbath rest.
   - Look at your plans for the coming week and make time to continue working on your habits.

Group Discussion Questions

READ MATTHEW 7:7–11.

1. Jesus encourages us to come to God and ask, believing that God loves to hear from us and will answer prayer. How does this help us to pray?

2. When Jesus says to ask, seek, and knock, those commands are in the present active imperative. In other words, *keep* asking; *keep* seeking; *keep* knocking. Why is persistence so important in prayer?

3. Jesus promises that God will answer prayer. Tim Keller says, "God always answers your prayers in precisely the way you want them to be answered if you knew everything he knew."[11] His answers are even better than our prayers. How does this encourage you?

4. The Bible encourages us to come to God with whatever is on our mind, and to pray about everything (1 Peter 5:6–7). How does this change how we approach prayer?

5. What are some approaches to prayer that you've found effective?

6. What questions do you have about prayer?

7. What should you pray about right now?

Worship and Belong

HABIT

Pursue worship and community within a church.

ASPIRATION

To live your life as part of God's people, both receiving from and contributing to the lives of other believers.

CHOOSE YOUR ACTIONS

Choose one or more of the following:

- If not part of a church, find some possible good churches near you.
- Attend church every week that you're able.
- Join a small group within the church.
- Pick someone in the church and look for a way to encourage him or her.

Introducing Habit #5:
Worship and Belong

WE'RE MEANT TO LIVE IN COMMUNITY with others who are pursuing God.

> **"If the church is central to God's purpose,
> as seen in both history and the gospel,
> it must surely also be central to our lives."
> (John Stott)**[1]

Welcome to your fifth habit.

Starting today, begin a new habit: worship and belong by participating in a local church. I'll give you some reasons why this is important and some tips on how to do this. As with other habits, you may already be doing this. If so, I'll challenge you to grow in practicing this habit.

THE BIG THREE

This habit, together with Habits 3 and 4, form the core habits of following Jesus:

- Engage the Bible (hear *from* God)
- Speak to God
- Worship and Belong (join God's people)

All the habits in this book are helpful. But the three core habits matter most. Whenever you feel overwhelmed, it's helpful to return to these core habits. They're foundational. We'll never outgrow them.

THE IMPORTANCE OF THE CHURCH

Many today think that the Christian life is personal—it's just you and God. The Bible presents a different picture. The focus of the Bible is God creating a community for Himself. In the Old Testament, this community was the nation of Israel. In the New Testament, it's about the church.

The church isn't an optional extra. It's at the very heart of God's purpose for us. When God changes us, He reorients us vertically (with Himself) and horizontally (with others). He adds us to His people, His family. He makes us

> a chosen race, a royal priesthood, a holy nation, a people for his own possession, that you may proclaim the excellencies of him who called you out of darkness into his marvelous light. Once you were not a people, but now you are God's people; once you had not received mercy, but now you have received mercy.
> (1 Peter 2:9–10)

Church is like a little outpost of heaven.

Church is all over the New Testament. As Christianity started, churches formed throughout the Roman world. As people followed Jesus, they entered into community within the church. The usual barriers that divided people, like race, gender, or economic division, were dissolved within the church. Church became family.

Although we usually read the Bible as individuals, it was written to groups. The letters of the New Testament, for instance, are primarily written to churches, not individuals. Even the letters to individuals, like 1 and 2 Timothy and Philemon, were meant to be overheard by the church. The Bible assumes that we're part of the family called the church.

You need the church, and the church needs you. The Bible tells us:

And let us consider how to stir up one another to love and good works, not neglecting to meet together, as is the habit of some, but encouraging one another, and all the more as you see the Day drawing near. (Heb. 10:24–25)

C. Michael Patton compares the church to a campfire:

Campfire designed by Megan Sheehan from The Noun Project. Illustration taken from *Now That I'm a Christian*. Copyright © 2014 by C. Michael Patton. Used by permission of Crossway.

These are all the activities we take part in when we are with other believers. What happens to a log when it is alone? The fire goes out. What happens when it is placed with other logs? The fire roars! In the body of Christ, the fire can only roar when we are together exercising these activities.[2]

WHAT TO DO TODAY

Make time for church. Look at your calendar for the coming week and set aside some time to attend a worship service.

In the next lesson days, I'll give you some tips on how to find a good church if you don't have one already.

If you already attend a church, consider how you will participate with that church this week. Make time for attending a small group meeting, connecting with a friend from church, or serving.

Then do what you can to practice your previous habits:

- **Speak with God**
- **Engage the Bible**
- **Rest and Refresh**—take some time to rest every day, and plan a day (or part of a day) of rest this week
- Continue to **Make Time** to work on these habits and on this book

Reflect and Respond

REVIEW

The church is central to God's purpose and, therefore, to our lives:

- The focus of the Bible is God creating a community for Himself.
- "Jesus came to create a people who would model what it means to live under his rule." The church is like an outpost of heaven.[3]
- "Our identity as Christians is found in Christ's new community."[4]

Pursuing worship and community within a church keeps our passion for God burning strong as we participate with other believers in the activities of:

- Fellowship
- Ordinances (baptism and the Lord's Supper)
- Encouragement
- Accountability
- Discipline
- Spiritual Gifts

CONSIDER

If you don't yet have a church: What excites and challenges you about finding a church community?

If you have a church: What activity—fellowship, the ordinances, encouragement, accountability, discipline, or spiritual gifts—fuels your desire to know more of God and His ways?

DISCUSS

1. Are you currently involved with a church?
2. How have you been involved?
3. What small action can you take today to experience or prepare for worship and community in your church?

What's a Good Church?

KNOW WHAT TO LOOK FOR in a good church, and how to know if it's time to leave.

We began a new habit in the last lesson: to get involved within a church. Today, we want to get practical and talk about what a good church looks like.

How does someone find a good church? Or how does someone even know if they're in a good church?

WHAT TO LOOK FOR

Finding a church is a big deal. What are some essential qualities of a good church?

Look for a church that:

- **Preaches the Bible.** Look for a church in which the Bible is treated as the highest authority. Look for a preacher who opens the Bible, explains a passage, and then applies it to the life of the congregation.

- **Talks about what Jesus did.** A lot. Good churches major in Jesus. They teach that God sent His Son Jesus to die in our place, and that we must respond by believing and following Him. Look for a church that not only explains this but applies it to all of life. Find a church that talks about, sings about, celebrates, and applies the gospel.
- **Gives you opportunities to grow.** Look for a church that invites you into community and mission. Look for one that gives you opportunities to serve, encourage, pray, and study with others in the church throughout the week. Don't look for a church that satisfies your desires; look for a church that calls you into service.
- **Follows the Bible's teaching on how to function as a church.** The Bible doesn't prescribe every detail on how to operate a church, but it does make some things clear. Churches should celebrate baptism and communion (the Lord's Supper). It should be led by godly leaders. It should practice church discipline (correcting sin in the life of the congregation and its members).
- **Embodies a healthy culture.** Look for a church that embodies grace, that incarnates "the biblical message in the relationships, vibe, feel, tone, values, priorities, aroma, honesty, freedom, gentleness, humility, cheerfulness—indeed, the total human reality of a church defined and sweetened by the gospel."[5]
- **On a practical level, look for a church that is close to where you live.** This will make it easier for you to participate.

These qualities are essential. Other things, like the style of music or the size of the church, are secondary. Focus on the essentials, and be relatively unconcerned about the incidentals.

If you are having a hard time finding a church, consider asking friends, or check the online directories of churches we've provided on our resource page (gospelforlife.com/church).

WHEN TO LEAVE

Leaving a church is a serious matter. If any of the following is true, then it's time to consider finding a new church:

- **When false teaching is accepted**—When a church begins to teach things that contradict the Bible on important issues, especially on key issues such as the gospel and the authority of Scripture, then it's time to consider leaving. Just make sure they're really teaching false doctrine on an important issue, rather than something you disagree with.[6]
- **When leaders are unqualified**—No leader is perfect, but when there is a pattern of abusive or ungodly leadership, then it's time to consider finding a new church.
- **When sin is tolerated**—It's good when church leaders deal gently with struggling Christians. It's bad, however, when sin is openly tolerated and uncorrected. When leaders tolerate sin within the church, it's time to consider leaving.

There are other good reasons to leave a church. While sometimes necessary, it's important to do so with a lot of prayer, open communication, and care. Sometimes people leave for the wrong reasons, like going to the next best, bigger thing.

Participate in your church with the greatest integrity. If you leave a church, leave with the greatest integrity. Be open, direct, humble, and sincere with your church leaders.

YOUR INVITATION

Choose one of the ideas below or come up with your own way to pursue worship and community in a church today.

If you're searching for a good church:

- Ask God to lead you to the church He desires for you.
- Ask friends or search online directories to find a church near you.
- Find service times and make time to attend a church near you this week.

If you're in a good church:

- Pray for the pastor and leaders of your church, the message and worship preparation for the weekly services, more of Jesus, an increase in serving, encouraging, praying, and studying with others, more baptisms, discipline and grace.
- Show up faithfully and look for ways to participate.
- Phone, send an email, meet up with, or send a note to someone in your church to let them know how they have been used by God in your life.
- Pray and prepare for a conversation of grace and truth with someone you have offended or someone who has hurt you.
- Ask about joining a small group or service team if you are not already participating in one.
- Come up with your own way to pursue worship and community in your church today.

If you're considering leaving your church:

- Pray for God's plans and purposes to be accomplished in your church, in the lives of those who appear to be at fault, in the leaders of your church, and in yourself.
- Ask God to reveal any contributing sin or blind spot in your thoughts, mindset, and behaviors.
- Pray and prepare for a conversation of grace and truth with your church leaders.

What about Online Church?

I remember calling my wife, Charlene, and our two children while traveling overseas. I was grateful for the telephone, and in later years for video calls. It helped to hear their voices and see them, but it still left me longing for more.

When I returned home, I was always overjoyed to be physically present with my wife and children again. No phone or video call came close.

In the same way, I'm grateful that we can stream our worship services and attend video meetings. When it's impossible to gather in person, I'm glad that we can stream services and stay in touch.

But it's not the same as gathering in person. God made us to be embodied beings, enjoying in-person relationships. He's designed the church to be an in-person community. Livestreams can be useful as a first step or in extenuating circumstances but can never replace in-person church. God's people are meant to gather.

In fact, the more that we move our lives on screens and devices, the more we need embodied church. We need in-person presence, encouragement, communication, and relationships.

In 2 John 12, the apostle John wrote, "Though I have much to write to you, I would rather not use paper and ink. Instead I hope to come to you and talk face to face, so that our joy may be complete." Letters were okay. In fact, John's letters are a gift that have served the church for two thousand years. But written letters are no substitute for personal presence, and neither is a prerecorded service or livestream. Stream an online service when you have no other choice, but remember there's no such thing as virtual church.

Reflect and Respond

REVIEW

A good church:

- Preaches the Bible
- Talks a lot about Jesus
- Gives you opportunities to grow
- Follows the Bible's teaching on running a church
- Embodies a healthy culture

To find a good church:

- Ask friends, neighbors, or coworkers
- Check online directories (found at gospelforlife.com/church)
- Focus on the essentials of a good church
- Don't be concerned about secondary things like size and music style

Bonus tip: This habit is easier when the church is close to where you live.

When to leave a church:

- False teaching is accepted
- Leaders display a pattern of abusive or ungodly leadership
- Sin is tolerated

To leave a church well:

- Pray, asking God to make His will clear to you
- Engage in open, honest, grace-filled communication with church leaders
- Express love and care to those you know in the church
- Refuse to gossip

CONSIDER

- Recall a time when you saw a church embody grace, or picture what it looks like when the reality of a church is defined and sweetened by the gospel.
- Pray for God to grow more of His grace in your thoughts, attitudes, and behaviors toward all who are part of the church you attend.

DISCUSS

1. Are you part of a *Bible-believing* church right now? If not, do you know of any in your area?
2. If you're part of a church but not as involved as you should be, what steps can you take to get more involved?
3. How can you encourage someone at your church today?

HABIT 5, LESSON 3

Why Worship?

WORSHIPING TOGETHER is one of the most important things we do.

On Sundays, when churches get together, it doesn't always look like much. Sometimes the gathering is humble, and sometimes the music is off-key.

Don't be fooled. Never underestimate what happens when God's people get together to worship.

WORSHIP MIRRORS HEAVEN

Our earthly meetings are a mirror of what's taking place in heaven. Some of the same things take place:

- Jesus meets with us. We always meet at God's invitation, and Jesus Himself promises to be with us when we gather (Matt. 18:20).
- Jesus speaks to us through His Word (Col. 3:16). As we teach, encourage, and sing together, Jesus speaks to His people.

- We respond with all of heaven in praising God. We join with the angels in praising God.

Our worship is a foretaste of the day we'll gather with all of God's people, praising the One who created and saved us.

Author Megan Hill writes:

> Your seat in church is more than it appears. It's more than the place where you lay your Bible and greet your friends. It's even more than the place where you regularly worship alongside the ten or a hundred or a thousand members of your local church.
>
> If you belong to Christ, your seat in church is not just a seat in church. It's a seat in heaven.[7]

When we worship, we're not just joining with other believers. We're worshiping with saints and angels in heaven.

WORSHIP SHAPES OUR SOULS

Worship also combines key habits that are essential for our spiritual growth. One writer, David Mathis, points out that worship combines the three core habits (the Bible, prayer, and fellowship) into one activity.[8]

Even better, we benefit from practicing these habits with others. Donald Whitney, a leading writer on spiritual disciplines, says:

> There's an element of worship and the Christian life that can never be experienced in private worship or by watching worship. There are some graces and blessings that our Father gives only when we "meet together" with other believers as His family.[9]

Practicing key habits in private is good, but something powerful happens when we practice these habits together. Jake Belder, a pastor and theologian, explains the power of worship in a series of tweets:

> Every so often, I get asked, "What feeds you spiritually? What works for you?" That question bugs me, for one, b/c nothing ever worked particularly well for me. "Quiet times," reading plans, they were all exhausting. But it also bugs me because the question assumes that you're entirely responsible for your own spirituality. And so you cycle through all manner of spiritual "techniques," just getting more exhausted and no more "spiritual." Nothing was more of a relief for me than discovering that the Church has already figured this all out for me. The Church gives me rituals and habits, rhythms and patterns, for nurturing my spirituality each day and throughout the year. But in this self-centered era, it takes a big step of faith to trust that the Church has more wisdom in these matters than you do. But when you do, recognizing the Spirit guides the Church in discerning how best to nurture its members' spirituality, it is so freeing. It's a gift to know the Church has 2000yrs of practices proven to form & shape you and that you don't have to figure it out for yourself.[10]

WORSHIP IS RIGHT

Jesus said that if we don't worship, the rocks will cry out (Luke 19:40). Worship is fitting and right for a few reasons:

- **God deserves worship.** We worship because God deserves it. To worship means to ascribe worth. To be human is to be a worshiper. We all ascribe worth to someone or something. Only God is worthy of our worship.
- **We need to worship.** We worship with other believers because we need to remember and practice the gospel. Worship

is what we do to have our "identity formed and refined as part of God's community, living under the testimony and authority of God's Word."[11]

- **Others need our worship.** Worshiping also encourages others. The Bible tells us that meeting together gives us a way to "stir up one another to love and good works" (Heb. 10:24–25). Worship also gives us an opportunity for "addressing one another in psalms and hymns and spiritual songs, singing and making melody to the Lord with your heart" (Eph. 5:19).

Worship extends beyond Sundays. God calls us to worship Him with our entire lives. But He also calls us to gather and worship with others. It's one of the most important things we do.

WHAT TO DO TODAY

As you look ahead to this weekend, begin to anticipate, and pray for, the time of worship with your church community. It's one of the most important things you'll do all week.

Reflect and Respond

REVIEW

Worship mirrors heaven

- By God's invitation, Jesus meets with us.
- Jesus speaks to us through His Word.
- We join all of heaven in praising God!

Worship shapes our souls

- The three core habits (Engage the Bible, Speak with God, and Worship and Belong) come together in one activity.
- We benefit! God releases blessings and graces on us as we practice these habits together with others.

Worship is right

- God deserves worship.
- We need to worship, to remember and practice the gospel.
- Our worship of God brings encouragement to those who are with us.

CONSIDER

- As you anticipate joining a worship service, what is the state of each part of your being—heart, mind, body, and soul?
- What do you need most today to be prepared for worship?

DISCUSS

Out of all the reasons to worship (worship mirrors heaven; worship shapes our souls; worship is right), which one strikes you the most? Why?

HABIT 5, LESSON 4

One Another

PURSUE "ONE ANOTHER" RELATIONSHIPS in the church.

It's easy to think of church as a Sunday worship service. As we discussed in the previous lesson, worship services are important. But the church is also a lot more.

The church is a community and a family in which we get to follow the "one another" commands of Scripture.

LOVE

John 13:34
A new commandment I give to you, that you love one another: just as I have loved you, you also are to love one another.

John 13:35
By this all people will know that you are my disciples, if you have love for one another.

John 15:12
This is my commandment, that you love one another as I have loved you.

John 15:17

These things I command you, so that you will love one another.

Romans 12:10

Love one another with brotherly affection. Outdo one another in showing honor.

Romans 16:16

Greet one another with a holy kiss.

1 Corinthians 16:20

Greet one another with a holy kiss.

2 Corinthians 13:12

Greet one another with a holy kiss.

Galatians 5:26

Let us not become conceited, provoking one another, envying one another.

Galatians 6:2

Bear one another's burdens, and so fulfill the law of Christ.

1 Peter 4:8

Above all, keep loving one another earnestly, since love covers a multitude of sins.

1 Peter 5:14

Greet one another with the kiss of love. Peace to all of you who are in Christ.

1 John 3:11

For this is the message that you have heard from the beginning, that we should love one another.

1 John 3:23

And this is his commandment, that we believe in the name of his Son Jesus Christ and love one another, just as he has commanded us.

1 John 4:7

Beloved, let us love one another, for love is from God, and whoever loves has been born of God and knows God.

1 John 4:11

Beloved, if God so loved us, we also ought to love one another.

1 John 4:12

No one has ever seen God; if we love one another, God abides in us and his love is perfected in us.

2 John 5

And now I ask you, dear lady—not as though I were writing you a new commandment, but the one we have had from the beginning—that we love one another.

SERVE

John 13:14

If I then, your Lord and Teacher, have washed your feet, you also ought to wash one another's feet.

Romans 15:14

I myself am satisfied about you, my brothers, that you yourselves are full of goodness, filled with all knowledge and able to instruct one another.

Galatians 5:13

For you were called to freedom, brothers. Only do not use your freedom as an opportunity for the flesh, but through love serve one another.

Ephesians 5:19

. . . addressing one another in psalms and hymns and spiritual songs, singing and making melody to the Lord with your heart . . .

Colossians 3:16

Let the word of Christ dwell in you richly, teaching and admonishing one another in all wisdom, singing psalms and hymns and spiritual songs, with thankfulness in your hearts to God.

1 Peter 4:9

Show hospitality to one another without grumbling.

1 Peter 4:10

As each has received a gift, use it to serve one another, as good stewards of God's varied grace.

PROMOTE UNITY

Romans 12:16

Live in harmony with one another. Do not be haughty, but associate with the lowly. Never be wise in your own sight.

Romans 14:13

Therefore let us not pass judgment on one another any longer, but rather decide never to put a stumbling block or hindrance in the way of a brother.

Romans 15:5

May the God of endurance and encouragement grant you to live in such harmony with one another, in accord with Christ Jesus.

Romans 15:7

Therefore welcome one another as Christ has welcomed you, for the glory of God.

1 Corinthians 11:33

So then, my brothers, when you come together to eat, wait for one another.

2 Corinthians 13:11

Finally, brothers, rejoice. Aim for restoration, comfort one another, agree with one another, live in peace; and the God of love and peace will be with you.

Ephesians 4:2

. . . with all humility and gentleness, with patience, bearing with one another in love . . .

Ephesians 4:32

Be kind to one another, tenderhearted, forgiving one another, as God in Christ forgave you.

Ephesians 5:21

. . . submitting to one another out of reverence for Christ.

Colossians 3:9

Do not lie to one another, seeing that you have put off the old self with its practices.

Colossians 3:13

. . . bearing with one another and, if one has a complaint against another, forgiving each other; as the Lord has forgiven you, so you also must forgive.

1 Peter 5:5

Likewise, you who are younger, be subject to the elders. Clothe yourselves, all of you, with humility toward one another, for "God opposes the proud but gives grace to the humble."

ENCOURAGE

1 Thessalonians 4:18

Therefore encourage one another with these words.

1 Thessalonians 5:11

Therefore encourage one another and build one another up, just as you are doing.

Hebrews 3:13

But exhort one another every day, as long as it is called "today," that none of you may be hardened by the deceitfulness of sin.

Hebrews 10:24

And let us consider how to stir up one another to love and good works . . .

Hebrews 10:25

. . . not neglecting to meet together, as is the habit of some, but encouraging one another, and all the more as you see the Day drawing near.

AVOID SINNING AGAINST ONE ANOTHER

1 Thessalonians 5:15

See that no one repays anyone evil for evil, but always seek to do good to one another and to everyone.

James 4:11

Do not speak evil against one another, brothers. The one who speaks against a brother or judges his brother, speaks evil against the law and judges the law. But if you judge the law, you are not a doer of the law but a judge.

James 5:9

Do not grumble against one another, brothers, so that you may not be judged; behold, the Judge is standing at the door.

CONFESS SIN

James 5:16

Therefore, confess your sins to one another and pray for one another, that you may be healed. The prayer of a righteous person has great power as it is working.

These commands necessitate relationships in which we intentionally serve each other. We need others, and they need us as well.

The goal for all of us should be to mentor and disciple others, helping them to grow. A good way to start is to practice the "one another" commands. Most of us feel inadequate to mentor others, but, with God's help, all of us can obey these commands. Look for a person or group of people, and get started.

The best place for this to happen is in small gatherings, often called small groups. It's where we switch from sitting in rows to sitting in circles. We begin to open our lives, to serve others, and to allow others to serve as well.

Obeying the one-another commands of Scripture is essential to the Christian life.

> **Being known means dropping the mask. It means letting people into our lives, including the messy parts. It also means loving, encouraging, supporting, and praying for others. It's inconvenient, and it takes time.**

BIBLICAL COMMUNITY IS INVITING AND SCARY

Obeying these commands is both inviting and scary at the same time.

It's inviting, because we all want relationships like this. We want to be known, loved, encouraged, supported, prayed for, received, and forgiven. When we experience these kinds of relationships, we feel alive. It feels like we could meet any challenge. We feel safe.

This is exactly what church should be like: a place where everyone is welcomed, warmly greeted, and loved.

But it's also scary. Being known means dropping the mask. It means letting people into our lives, including the messy parts. It also means loving, encouraging, supporting, and praying for others. It's inconvenient, and it takes time.

These kinds of relationships also involve risk. What if we open ourselves up, and we're disappointed? The truth is that this will probably happen. Pursue this kind of relationship anyway. It's worth the inconvenience and the possibility—even likelihood—of getting hurt.

Larry Crabb describes what this can look like:

> When members of a spiritual community reach a sacred place of vulnerability and authenticity, something is released. Something good begins to happen. An appetite for holy things is stirred. For just a moment, the longing to know God becomes intense, stronger than all other passions, worth whatever price must be paid for it. Spiritual togetherness, what I call *connecting*, creates movement: *Togetherness* in Christ encourages *movement* toward Christ.[12]

FOR TODAY

Most churches include small gatherings as part of their ministry. They may be called by different names (life groups or community groups, for instance). They are great opportunities to practice the "one another" commands.

- **If you are part of a small gathering** that practices these "one another" commands, well done! Take a small step to live out a "one another" command with someone in your group today.
- **If you are part of a church but haven't joined a small gathering**, find out how you can join one. Visit the church website to

see if they have small groups available, or contact the church to find out how to join one.

- **If you aren't part of a church**, then look for a church that has the essential qualities of a good church (see Habit 5, Lesson 2) and offers small groups.

Reflect and Respond

REVIEW

Church is . . .

- a total identity that is ours in Christ
- a community and family
- intentional relationships in which we live out "one another" commands
- where we are known, loved, encouraged, supported, prayed for, received, forgiven
- inconvenient, time-consuming, at times disappointing and painful, but always worth it

Some "one another" commands:

- Greet one another (Rom. 16:16)
- Encourage one another (1 Thess. 4:18)
- Forgive one another (Col. 3:13)
- Build one another up (1 Thess. 5:11)
- Serve one another (Gal. 5:13)
- Love one another (John 13:34)
- Bear one another's burdens (Gal. 6:2)
- Encourage one another (Heb. 10:25)
- Meet with one another (Heb. 10:25)
- Be kind to one another, tenderhearted, forgiving one another (Eph. 4:32)
- Welcome one another (Rom. 15:7)
- Care for one another (1 Cor. 12:25)

- Show hospitality to one another (1 Peter 4:9)
- Pray for one another (James 5:16)
- Confess your sins to one another (James 5:16)

CONSIDER

1. Which "one another" command is most challenging for you to do?
2. Which of the "one another" commands is hard for you to receive from someone else?

DISCUSS

1. Have you ever experienced a community where the "one another" commands of Scripture were practiced?
2. If you're not part of a small gathering of believers, what steps can you take to join one?
3. What small step can you take to practice a "one another" command today?

HABIT 5, LESSON 5

A Game Plan
for Church

BE INTENTIONAL before, during, and after you attend church.

You'd think it would be easy to walk into a church gathering. It's not.

Every worship service is an opportunity to encounter God, encourage others, and advance God's mission. We need a game plan when so much is at stake!

Here's what we can do before, during, and after we meet together at church.

BEFORE CHURCH

Let's not overlook an important step: plan to be there, whenever possible, every week. Unless we make worship a priority, other activities will crowd it out. Tony Payne writes:

> What really stops many of us from turning up more frequently to church is a failure to grasp just how vital the "ministry of turning

up" really is. One of the most important acts of love and encouragement we can all engage in is the powerful encouragement of just being there—because every time I walk into church, I am wearing a metaphorical t-shirt that says, "God is important to me, and you are important to me." And on the back it says, "And that's why I wouldn't dream of missing this."

Similarly, when we stay away for no good reason one week out of three (or more), we send the opposite message.[13]

It's important to show up. Beforehand, prepare yourself. This includes getting enough rest the night before, leaving on time, and praying for God to work during the service.

Preparation is important for worship.

DURING CHURCH

If you go to the gym, you've probably heard about the importance of engaging your core. You can exercise without using your core, but you won't get the same results.

In the same way, when you gather at church, engage your core. Refuse to sleepwalk through worship. Think about the words you sing. Let your heart engage with the truths you encounter. Listen to the sermon with expectancy. Don't run out immediately after; strike up a conversation with someone instead.

Sam Allberry says, "It is almost impossible to overstate the positive impact we can have on others if we are coming looking for ways in which to be an encouragement."[14]

Expect to encounter God when you worship at church. Expect God to use you. Ask for His help. Do everything in your power to worship Him and to encourage others.

AFTER CHURCH

When you leave church, make some time to reflect on what you experienced. Review the Scripture, and ask God to reveal any action that you should take. If you encountered anyone who needs prayer, make a note to pray for them that week.

Commit to pray for the ministry of your church. Pray for the leaders and for others who are part of that church community. Ask God to continue to work and begin to pray for the coming week.

Annie Dillard once advised people to wear crash helmets to church. "The churches are children playing on the floor with their chemistry sets, mixing up a batch of TNT to kill a Sunday morning," she wrote.[15] Dillard reminds us that, as we gather in church, we are worshiping a holy and powerful God who is alive and holding the entire universe together. We proclaim a message that can change lives for eternity. We engage in spiritual battle. We sometimes forget how important and serious it is to worship God together. It's important to take worship seriously before, during, and after we attend church.

OVER TO YOU

First, take a look at your calendar today and prioritize the "ministry of showing up."

Second, determine what you need to do, or change, in order to be present and prepared for your time with God and others. Start with one small change and grow from there.

Then check in on your previous habits. Do what you can with each one to:

- **Speak with God.** Hand over today's needs, anxieties, and joys to God throughout your day.

- **Engage the Bible**. Pick up and continue where you are with your plan for reading or listening to the Bible.
- **Rest and Refresh**. Take a few moments to identify the presence or absence of wholeheartedness in your body, heart, mind, and soul. Plan one small restorative action for today and schedule time for a day, or partial day, of rest this week.
- **Make Time**. Continue to make time for your habits and for this book.

Reflect and Respond

REVIEW

The "ministry of showing up" is vital to encounter God, encourage others, and advance God's mission.

GET YOUR GAME ON!

Select an action from the list below or come up with your own ideas to create a simple game plan for church.

Before church, prepare for worship by:

- getting enough rest the night before
- leaving on time
- praying for God to work during the service

During church, engage in worship by:

- expecting to encounter and hear from God
- asking for God to help you worship
- thinking about the words you sing
- allowing the truths you encounter to challenge your mind and emotions
- listening to the sermon, expecting God's Word to speak to you
- talking with someone about what you were challenged or encouraged by after the service
- encouraging someone else

After church, extend worship by:

- reflecting on what you experienced
- reviewing the Scripture passage
- asking God to reveal any action that you should take
- making a note to pray for any needs you became aware of
- praying for God to work in and through church leaders, ministries, community and individual needs in the coming week

CONSIDER

1. Do you think of worshiping God together as dangerous? Why or why not?
2. Looking at the components of a game plan for church before, during, and after:
   - What are you doing really well?
   - What suggestions are new to you?
   - What ideas challenge you?

DISCUSS

1. What small step will you take before church to prepare for worship?
2. What small step will you take during church to engage in worship?
3. What small step will you take after church to extend worship?
4. What are your plans for worshiping with others in the coming week?

HABIT #5: WORSHIP AND BELONG

Review

HABIT 5 COMBINES THREE of the most important habits in the Christian life. When we pursue worship and fellowship within a church, three things happen:

- we absorb God's Word
- we speak to God in prayer
- we worship God and enjoy fellowship with believers

Here's a summary of what we covered.

- We introduced a new habit: pursue worship and fellowship within a church.
- Our passion for God is like a campfire: solitary faith grows cold by itself but, placed together with other believers, our faith is fueled and sustained.
- Tips on how to spot a good church: it preaches the Bible, talks about Jesus, gives opportunities to grow, follows the Bible in

how it runs, and embodies a healthy culture of grace.

- We looked at some reasons why it's important for us to worship. Worship mirrors heaven, shapes our soul, and is right.
- We covered biblical commands for how we're supposed to relate to each other within the church. The "one another" commands provide practical ways to practice costly grace and loving truth-telling.
- We expanded worship and community to include what happens before, during, and after we participate in church.

RESOURCES

Visit gospelforlife.com/church for resources on this habit.

CONSIDER

Think about your experience with this habit.

- What went well for you?
- Where did you succeed, even a little bit?
- What can you celebrate?

WHAT TO DO TODAY

Review yesterday's responses for your game plan for church and take a small action to put your game plan into action.

Then, do what you can to practice your previous habits:

- **Speak with God.** Tell Him what's on your mind today.
- **Engage the Bible.** Keep reading and allowing Scripture to shape your mind.
- **Rest and Refresh.** Get the rest you need to function well.

- **Make Time**. Take a look at the coming week. Anticipate challenges. Then decide where and when you will commit to practice your habits and continue to work through this book.

Group Discussion Questions

READ HEBREWS 10:24–25.

1. According to Hebrews 10:25, people were trying to skip out on church two thousand years ago. Why do you think it's so easy to neglect church?

2. The writer to the Hebrews says that participation in church is one of the key ways that we're encouraged (and that we encourage others) to continue in the faith. How does church help us with this?

3. What are some ways that you've been encouraged in your faithfulness to God through church?

4. The writer also expresses urgency: "all the more as you see the Day drawing near." How does church help to prepare us for the return of Jesus Christ?

5. What are some of your favorite "one another" commands in Scripture? Which ones do you think deserve more attention?

6. What are some approaches to staying faithful in worship and fellowship that you've found effective?

7. What questions do you have about this habit?

Care for Your Body

HABIT

Take action each day to care for your body.

ASPIRATION

To care for your body for God's glory and so that you can love and serve others.

CHOOSE YOUR ACTIONS

Choose one or more of the following:

- Eat slowly. Savor every bite. Really enjoy food when you eat.
- Pay attention to hunger signals, and pay attention to when you're hungry and full.
- Learn how to cook a tasty, nutritious new dish.
- Buy a cookbook of nutritious recipes you're able to cook.
- Brainstorm a list of physical activities you enjoy and choose one to try.
- Set an alarm to remind you to get outside and go for a walk each day.

Introducing Habit #6:
Care for Your Body

GOD MADE US EMBODIED CREATURES. He calls us to care for every part of our lives, including our bodies.

Welcome to a new habit: care for your body.

Beginning today, take action each day to care for your body.

Don't worry! I'm not talking about starting a fad diet or killer workout plan. The goal is healthy behaviors for eating, activity, and rest.

Of course, I encourage you to keep doing what you can to practice your previous habits too, especially the core habits of engaging the Bible, speaking to God, and worshiping and belonging.

THE BODY MATTERS

I occasionally hear a quote: "We are not human beings having a spiritual experience. We are spiritual beings having a human experience."[1]

It sounds good, right? Human things sometimes seem so, well, human. We have to sleep, brush our teeth, and use the bathroom. It's easy to start to think that the most important part of ourselves is the spiritual part, and that the body is just a shell for what matters.

Here's the thing, though: this is not what the Bible teaches about what it means to be human. In the Bible we find that:

- **God created us with bodies,** and called our creation very good (Gen. 1:26–31). Our physicality is part of God's design for us.
- **Our bodies are not our temporary home.** God promises to raise them after we die, so that we will spend eternity in our resurrected bodies (1 Cor. 15:53).
- **Most importantly, God the Son Himself became human.** Jesus is both God and man, and will have a body throughout eternity (1 Tim. 2:5).

Our bodies matter. God made us embodied creatures.

WHAT THIS MEANS

Theologian Millard Erickson writes:

> Humans are to be treated as unities. Their spiritual condition cannot be dealt with independently of their physical and psychological condition, and vice versa. . . . *The Christian who desires to be spiritually healthy will give attention to such matters as diet, rest, and exercise.* Any attempt to deal with people's spiritual condition apart from their physical condition and mental and emotional state will be only partially successful, as will any attempt to deal with human emotions apart from people's relationship to God. . . .

The gospel is an appeal to the whole person. It is significant that Jesus in his incarnation became fully human, for he came to redeem the whole of what we are.[2]

Bottom line: God cares about redeeming all of you, including your body.

SOME IDEAS

To translate this important truth into action, begin with an action from the suggestions below or come up with your own idea.

- **Get a little extra sleep or rest.** Take a nap, go to bed a little early, or sleep in a little later.
- **Move.** Take a walk, go to the gym, hop on your bike, or swim. Find a physical activity you enjoy and do it.
- **Eat tasty, nutritious food slowly.** Pick up some fresh fruit or vegetables from a local market, or grill your favorite cut of meat. Whether a snack or meal, eat slowly.
- **Drink water first.** Reach for water first before caloric and caffeinated beverages (juice, soda, tea, coffee, iced tea, and energy drinks).

Your body matters to God. I can't wait to explore this with you more, and to talk about how to build this habit into your life.

Reflect and Respond

REVIEW

What the Bible teaches about our bodies:

- God created us with bodies and called our creation very good.
- Our bodies are not our temporary home; we will spend eternity in our resurrected bodies.
- God the Son (Jesus) became human and is embodied for eternity.

Theologian Millard Erickson is right: "The Christian who desires to be spiritually healthy will give attention to such matters as diet, rest, and exercise."

Suggested actions to care for your body:

- Increase sleep or rest.
- Move more.
- Eat some nutritious, whole food slowly.
- Drink water first.

DISCUSS

1. Are you tempted to think that God cares more about your soul than your body?
2. What Scriptures, thoughts, or feelings cause you to remember God's care for your body?
3. How often do you typically think about God's care for your body?
4. What action will you take today to care for your body?

HABIT 6, LESSON 2

Two Lies, One Truth

WE ARE BOTH BODY AND SOUL, and will be for eternity.

The last lesson introduced you to a new habit: care for your body.

We're about to get practical about how to do this. But first, let's take a moment and consider *who you aren't*, and more importantly, *who you really are*. There's a lot of misunderstanding out there in the world and in the church, so it's crucial we understand what the Bible says about the importance of both the body and soul.

I've noticed two common lies about our bodies, as well as one truth that is important for us to understand and apply.

LIE #1: OUR BODIES MATTER, NOT OUR SOULS

Some believe that we don't have a soul. They believe that we're just a collection of chemical and electrical reactions. You're just physical matter. No soul. End of story.

That's not what the Bible teaches.

You're more than a body. You were made in the image of God. God Himself breathed life into us (Gen. 2:7). You have a soul that will live even when your body dies (Matt. 10:28; 2 Cor. 5:8).

In fact, Paul commands us to pay even more attention to the state of our soul than our bodies, even though both are important (1 Tim. 4:8–10). One writer says:

> Physical exercise does have "some value." It pays off health-wise. For this reason I jog and lift weights and minimize my intake of doughnuts and Twinkies. But the value of physical exercise is limited. Arnold Schwarzenegger will not take his massive biceps or cannonball deltoids into eternity—or probably even to the grave. But there is no doubt that physical exercise has profited him.[3]

But training for godliness has unlimited benefits both in this world and in the coming world—"holding promise for both the present life and the life to come" (NIV)—because the Christian life is one life. The godliness that comes from training in God's Word has unlimited value for every environment.

Our bodies matter, but our souls matter even more. Don't buy the lie that you're only a body. Your soul matters.

LIE #2: OUR SOULS MATTER, NOT OUR BODIES

Some people, including Christians, go to the other extreme. They believe the soul matters, but they downplay the body. They think that our bodies are a container—or, even worse, a prison—for our souls. The important part of us is spiritual. The body is merely a shell for what really matters.

This is not a new lie. It goes all the way back to New Testament times. As we've already seen in a previous lesson, God made us embodied creatures. Matter is good. Our bodies are good. God created earth, and He created us as humans with a body and soul.

Your soul is not trapped in your body. **Your body and soul belong together. It's what God intended.**

If we believe one of the two lies we just described, we won't care for our bodies in the way that truly honors God's right way of living.

Instead, here's a truth we can believe and apply as we follow Jesus.

THE TRUTH: OUR BODIES AND SOULS BOTH MATTER

The Bible's view of who we are is completely different. God made us as embodied souls, and said that this is very good. Our bodies and souls will be separated for a brief time after our death, but not forever. Our bodies will be resurrected, and we will spend eternity as embodied creatures.

Not only that, but eternity will be physical. Christians are headed for a new earth (Rev. 21:1–4). We will enjoy the earth for eternity in God's presence. It will be even better than what God originally created.

Our bodies and souls both matter to God, and both will matter into eternity.

God's creation, everything made by Him, is very good, and that matters—a lot! Mike Wittmer writes:

Enjoy creation! Our first responsibility as humans is to find pleasure in our Father's world. . . .

Where are the places you connect with God's creation? It may be sinking your fingers into a mound of topsoil, jogging down a tree-lined avenue, or plopping a lure into some promising weeds at water's edge. Wherever and whenever it happens for you, take a moment to thank God for his beautiful creation. Thank him for putting you here. Enjoy, celebrate, and, yes, even indulge in this, your Father's world.[4]

WHAT TO DO TODAY

Get outside! Give your body and soul the opportunity to enjoy the physical world that God has created.

Need a bigger challenge? Continue the practice of caring for your body that you started in Lesson 1 and notice how the experience changes as you continue to practice your habit.

Enjoy life as an embodied soul today. It will be good practice for eternity.

Reflect and Respond

REVIEW

- Lie #1: Our bodies matter, not our souls.
- Lie #2: Our souls matter, not our bodies.

If we believe *either one* of these two lies, we won't care for our bodies in a way that honors God's right way of living.

Truth: Our bodies and souls both matter.

- Christians are bound for a new earth where God will be present.
- We're designed to find joy in being alive—body and soul—with God in His good creation. It's good practice for eternity!

CONSIDER

- Do you think of your body as something good that God has created? Why or why not?
- As you take action to care for your body, how can you remind yourself that God cares about your entire being, including your body?

DISCUSS

1. When do you feel tempted to act as though "my soul matters, not my body"?
2. How does a small action of caring for your body connect to the truth that your body and soul both matter to God?
3. How do you feel when you think of spending eternity enjoying God's creation as both body and soul?
4. What action will you take to care for your body today?

HABIT 6, LESSON 3

Why Care for Your Body?

WHAT'S YOUR MOTIVATION for caring for your body? Before getting started, let's check in.

- How are you doing with taking action to care for your body?
- Have you landed on an action that is both enjoyable and doable in the circumstances of your life?

Now let's look at why caring for our bodies is an essential part of our spiritual life and growth, and how that connects with our motivation.

START WITH WHY

In an article on DesiringGod.org, Stacy Reaoch argues that our reasons for looking after our body go deeper than physical appearance. "Exercise can be a good and healthy discipline to invest in when done for the right reasons," she writes.[5]

Reaoch focuses on one benefit of exercise she enjoys: it helps her manage her emotions and drives her into greater relationship with God.

I've learned that as I keep the discipline of heading to the gym or going out for a jog, I'm rewarded with a happier spirit and an increase in energy. God often uses exercise as a means to turn my sullen mood toward a joyful one.

When her body isn't dragging her down, she writes, she finds it less difficult to delight in the Lord. Don't miss the connection. The time that Reaoch invests in physical exercise moves her soul into deeper relational delight in God.

Exercise is both body *and* soul care. The same benefits apply to other forms of caring for our bodies, like eating slowly and rest.

Caring for our bodies is part of stewarding the bodies God has given us. It keeps our bodies in good condition so that we can serve God and others. It helps to give us energy and keep our minds alert. "Regular exercise is worth so much more than a flat stomach or a smaller waist size," Reaoch says. "It can be a pathway toward deeper love and joy in our heavenly Father."

What's your motivation to care for your body?

Take a few moments to think about the reasons God wants you to care for your body. Make a note, and keep reminding yourself of these reasons.

FOR TODAY

Receive a gift of grace and joy from God today as you practice an action to care for your body:

- move
- eat good food slowly
- rest
- drink water first
- get outdoors and enjoy God's good creation

Your body matters.

Reflect and Respond

REVIEW

Caring for your body is both body and soul care. Growing a habit of caring for your body is integral to your life:

- It's part of stewarding the body God has given you.
- It helps keep your body in good condition so that you can serve God and others.
- It helps to give you energy and keep your mind alert.
- It can be a path to deeper love and joy in God.

CONSIDER

What's your motivation to care for your body? In Habit 1, Lesson 3, we explored your motivation for wanting to grow. We asked:

Picture the future you. Where do you want to be? How do you want to feel? How will your life have changed? Try to describe your hopes and goals in as much detail as possible.

I want to be . . .
I want to feel . . .
I want to change . . .

As you think about your response back then:

- Do the answers reflect the desires and motivations for both your soul and body?

- What would you add, change, or revise to integrate more of your body into your hopes for the future?

DISCUSS

1. Which of the reasons to care for your body resonate most with you?
2. Are there any other reasons why you want to care for your body?
3. What are some of your hopes for your physical health in the future?
4. What action will you take today to move, eat, or rest as you care for your body?

HABIT 6, LESSON 4

Care for Your Body with Food

ASK FOR GOD'S HELP to use the gift of food well.

It can be confusing to figure out what to eat. So many books, so many opinions, so much conflicting advice!

How can we sort through the clutter and learn how to care for our bodies with the food we eat?

THE BIBLE AND FOOD

Surprisingly, the Bible is full of references to food. In Genesis, we learn that food is given as a gift to enjoy (Gen. 2:16–17). It's what Satan first used to tempt us to disobey God (Gen. 3:1–7), so it's not surprising that it's something many people struggle with today. When God calls Israel to Himself, He talks a lot about the food they should eat, and He even provides food for them. God gave the Passover meal to Israel (Ex. 12) and the communion meal to His church (Matt. 26:17–30). Food is everywhere!

Food shows up everywhere in Jesus' ministry. New Testament scholar Robert Karris says: "In Luke's Gospel Jesus is either going to a meal, at a meal, or coming from a meal."[6] If you remove food from the Gospels, they would be a lot shorter.

Food is also in our future. When Jesus returns, we'll enjoy a wedding meal with Him (Rev. 19:6–9).

Clearly, God gave us food as a gift to enjoy. "Go, eat your bread with joy, and drink your wine with a merry heart" (Eccl. 9:7). It's a way to connect and build relationships with people. Food is part of eternity.

I love how Robert Farrar Capon reminds us of God's goodness and delight in what He has created:

> He *likes* onions, therefore they are. The fit, the colors, the smell, the tensions, the tastes, the textures, the lines, the shapes are a response, not to some forgotten decree that there may as well be onions as turnips, but to His present delight—His intimate and immediate joy in all you have seen, and in the thousand other wonders you do not even suspect.[7]

Food keeps us alive, but that's not all it does. "Its *eternal* purpose is to furnish our sensibilities against the day when we shall sit down at the heavenly banquet and see how gracious the Lord is."[8]

Food is a gift. And yet, as with all things that are created, food needs to be kept in its place. God, not food, is what ultimately satisfies (Matt. 4:4; John 6:35).

THE HEART OF EATING

We'll get to the how of eating in a minute. The really tough part, though, isn't the how. It's our hearts.

In her book *Full*, Asheritah Ciuciu describes some of her struggles with compulsive eating patterns. She realizes that these patterns aren't about the food itself. They're about her heart. "Until we deal with the heart issue of seeking fullness in food instead of God, our eating habits will never change," she writes.[9]

Our ongoing struggle in all of life is to enjoy God's gifts without loving them too much. Satan's strategy is to take God's good gifts (such as food), weaponize them, and turn them against us. Our call is to enjoy these gifts the way God intends, to submit these gifts to Him, and to find our ultimate satisfaction in Him.

Bottom line: food is often a spiritual battlefield! That thought can be uncomfortable to our Western mentality and cause us to skip right to the practical. As Christians who desire to follow Jesus, don't neglect the spiritual dimension! Ask for God's help. Ask Him to help you find the joy He intends in food and to find your ultimate satisfaction in Him. Cultivate your love for Jesus.

Remember that you're not alone: if you have turned to Jesus in faith and repentance, He has promised His Spirit to help you.

THE HOW OF EATING

What are some practical steps we can take to eat well?

I like Michael Pollan's advice in *Food Rules*: "Eat food. Not too much. Mostly plants."[10] Let's break that down:

- **Eat food**—real food, stuff that your grandmother and great-grandmother would have eaten, food that's minimally processed and nutritious.
- **Eat (more) plants**—North American diets tend to be heavy on refined sugar, fats, grains, and meat. Adding more well-

grown plants, from healthy soil, adds color, taste, and variety to our plate. Not only does it taste great, it also boosts needed nutrients, helping our bodies function and perform better.

- **Not too much**—enough to satisfy and fuel you, but not enough to negatively impact your health.

Be sure to check the tips and resources in the Reflect and Respond section for this lesson.

WHAT TO DO TODAY

1. Remember that God cares about your body, including what you eat. He gives us food as a sign of His love and care for us. Enjoy your food.
2. Notice what you feel or don't feel, without judgment, as you eat today. Bring your feelings honestly to God.
3. Ask God for His help to enjoy your food in a way that contributes to both your spiritual and physical health.

Reflect and Respond

REVIEW

- God gave us food as a gift to enjoy.
- Connect and build relationships with people around food like Jesus did.
- Food is part of eternity.
- Cultivate the spiritual dimension of eating. Ask God for help to find ultimate satisfaction in Him and joy in His gift of food.

THE HOW OF EATING:

- Eat real food
- Eat (more) plants
- Not too much

RESOURCES

Check out some resources on caring for your body with food at gospelforlife.com/body.

CONSIDER

How much time do you spend eating each meal?

It takes twenty minutes for the satiety signal to travel from our gut to our brain—in our "always on" world, that often means that the message comes too late—we've eaten and moved on before our mind is aware that we are full. The solution? **Slow down to eat.** Here's how:

- Make time: 20–30 minutes for small meals, more for larger meals.
- Drink plenty of water before, during, and after each meal.
- Put down utensils between mouthfuls.
- Chew each mouthful a set number of times before swallowing.
- Use small plates, or try chopsticks for utensils.
- Turn off devices and visual media while eating.
- Have meaningful conversation with others.

- Find a slow-eating buddy to pace yourself. Picky eaters, talkative people, and toddlers are often excellent. Alternately, challenge a family member, friend, or colleague to eat slowly with you.

DISCUSS

1. Food is a major theme in Scripture and a gift from God. Why do you think we sometimes tend to overlook this theme?
2. Asheritah Ciuciu argues, "We can't solve a spiritual problem with a physical solution."[11] How is what we eat a spiritual issue?
3. How will you treat your eating as a spiritual issue?
4. "Eat food. Mostly plants. Not too much." What do you find helpful about this advice? What do you find difficult?
5. What action will you take to care for your body with food today?

HABIT 6, LESSON 5

Care for Your Body with Movement

WHAT WE DO WITH OUR BODIES—including exercise—matters to God and to us. The state of our body affects the state of our souls.

My wife, Char, loves to exercise. Give her a foam roller, stretch bands, and free weights, and she's in her happy place.

I go to the gym, but not because I love it. I prefer outside activities like walking and biking, sometimes even running. When I get busy, I'm tempted to see exercise as an interruption rather than something essential.

If you like the gym like Char, go for it. I admire you, and I'm a little bit jealous. But for the rest of us, here's some encouraging news:

You don't need to buy special outfits or equipment, and you can start right where you are—in your office, your kitchen, your backyard, your neighborhood. There's only one basic instruction: Take any and every opportunity to move, in any way possible, at whatever speed you like, for any amount of time. Do what makes you feel good; stop doing what makes you feel bad.[12]

In other words, *move*. Go to the gym if you like, but if you don't, find another way. Find something you like, and get your body moving.

AS SIMPLE AS A WALK

When I was growing up, my mother faced a lot of stress, and not just because she has me as a son. She was a single mother of four children with more bills than money. She worked full-time and drove home every night to prepare dinner and manage the household. Life was not easy.

Her doctor gave her advice: every day, no matter how much work she had on her desk, and no matter how bad the weather, she should get up from the desk and go for a walk. She did. Life was still hard, but the daily walks helped her cope.

Dr. JoAnn E. Manson of the Harvard Medical School says:

If there was a pill that people could take that would nearly cut in half the risk of stroke, diabetes, heart disease, reduce the risk of cognitive decline, depression, reduce stress, improve emotional well-being—everyone would be clamoring to take it, it would be flying off the shelf. But that pill, that magic potion, really is available to everyone in the form of thirty minutes a day of brisk walking.[13]

Dr. Manson reports that walking is one of the main prescriptions she dispenses for people with various emotional, mental, and physical ailments.

Other activities work too: biking, swimming, stretching, dancing, gardening, soccer, squash, running, and aerobics, for instance. It's amazing what a little movement can do.

A THEOLOGY OF EXERCISE

In the first lesson on this habit, I quoted theologian Millard Erickson:

> The Christian who desires to be spiritually healthy will give attention to such matters as diet, rest, and exercise. Any attempt to deal with people's spiritual condition apart from their physical condition and mental and emotional state will be only partially successful, as will any attempt to deal with human emotions apart from people's relationship to God.[14]

What we do with our bodies—including exercise—matters to God and to us. The state of our body affects the state of our souls. We're meant to honor God with our bodies.

GRACE UPON GRACE

You may like what I'm saying. Or, it may make you feel guilty, annoyed, or skeptical. After all, many of us may have failed to treat our bodies as well as we could have.

We can't change the past, but can know that God gives grace to those who've failed. "For from his fullness we have all received, grace upon grace" (John 1:16). Jesus meets us right where we are, even in the middle of failure, and gives us all the grace we need and more.

Rest in that grace, and move as you're able. Find something you like to do, and do what you can. What you do with your body matters.

Author and pastor David Mathis writes:

When my life is joyfully active, and not sedentary—when my legs and arms feel strong, and the truth feels strong and clear that the happier life comes from activity, not passivity—I'm more ready to spring into action to help others. My whole orientation on the world is not passive, but active. Ready to move. Ready to respond. Ready to hear. Ready to help. Ready to love.[15]

Reflect and Respond

REVIEW

- You don't need to go to the gym if you don't want to. Just move more. Find some activity you like and do more of that.
- Simple exercise like walking can make a big difference in your mental, spiritual, and physical health.
- God made us as embodied beings. What we do with our bodies matters to Him.
- God gives grace for those who fail or struggle.

CONSIDER

Michelle Segar writes, "Take any and every opportunity to move, in any way possible, at whatever speed you like, for any amount of time."[16]

Think about the different kinds of movement:

- Stretching
- Walking
- Running
- Biking
- Weight training
- Swimming
- Dancing
- Gardening
- Soccer
- Football
- Frisbee golf
- Golf
- Skiing

Add your own ideas to this list.

DISCUSS

1. What kinds of movement do you enjoy? How can you build more of the movements you like into your life?
2. What are some of the benefits of movement (mental, spiritual, and physical) that you've experienced?
3. God created our bodies, and they belong to Him. How does this affect your view of how you eat and move?
4. How can you receive God's grace today, even if you've failed in how you've cared for your body?

HABIT #6: CARE FOR YOUR BODY

Review

IN THIS HABIT, we've looked at the importance of caring for our bodies. When we look at the Bible, we find that:

- God made us embodied creatures, and He calls us to care for every part of our lives, including our bodies.
- Our bodies and souls matter to God. Our souls and resurrected bodies will exist for eternity.

We responded to these truths by:

- exploring our motivation for caring for our bodies.
- asking for God's help to use the gift of food well.
- looking for ways to move our bodies.

We considered suggestions and practical resources for caring for our bodies so that we:

- Get a little extra sleep or rest
- Eat tasty, nutritious food slowly
- Move and exercise

RESOURCES

Visit gospelforlife.com/body for resources on this habit.

CONSIDER

Think about your experience in caring for your body.

- What went well for you?
- Where did you succeed, even a little bit?
- What can you celebrate?

WHAT TO DO TODAY

1. Care for your body. Take action to do a little more, a little better to care for your body today.
2. Then, do what you can to:

   - make time for your lessons and habits in the coming week
   - rest for a brief time each day and work toward a full day of Sabbath rest once a week
   - read or listen to the Bible
   - pray
   - pursue worship and community in a church

Group Discussion Questions

READ PSALM 139:13-16.

1. In Genesis 1, God creates everything—including man and woman—and pronounces creation "very good" (Gen. 1:31). He made us to be physical creatures in a physical world. How does that shape how we see our bodies?

2. In Psalm 139, the psalmist praises God for how his body was created. He calls our bodies "fearfully and wonderfully made." What aspect of the human body causes you to marvel at God's handiwork?

3. First Timothy 4:8 affirms the benefits of exercise, while acknowledging that the benefits will only last so long because we die. What are some of the benefits of exercise that you've noticed?

4. God made us as embodied beings, and He will one day transform and glorify our bodies. Why do you think some Christians tend to downplay the importance of the body?

5. What are some approaches to caring for your body that you've found effective?

6. What challenges have you experienced with this habit?

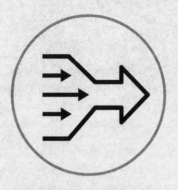

Simplify and Prioritize

HABIT

Look for ways to simplify your life in order to keep your focus on the main thing.

ASPIRATION

To release distractions so you can focus on what matters most.

CHOOSE YOUR ACTIONS

Choose one or more of the following:

- Create a list of distractions in your life.
- Delete distracting apps from your phone.
- Make a list of "most important activities" that you want to prioritize in your life.
- Consider quitting something that isn't a priority in your life.

Introducing Habit #7:
Simplify and Prioritize

KEEP YOUR FOCUS on the main thing.

You may be surprised to learn that for this penultimate habit, I'm asking you to do less!

I designed the first habit to help you prepare to make changes in your life. Habits 2 to 6 are meant to help you build key behaviors in your life, including the three core habits (engaging the Bible, speaking to God, and worshiping and belonging). The final two habits are meant to help you maintain these habits for the rest of your life, and to get back on track when needed.

Starting today, look for ways to simplify your life in order to keep your focus on the main thing.

THE WEIGHTIER MATTERS

We tend to overcomplicate things. Given enough time, we tend to lose focus on the main thing and add a bunch of peripheral things. Jesus addressed this concern. Speaking to religious leaders, he said:

> "Woe to you, scribes and Pharisees, hypocrites! For you tithe mint and dill and cumin, and have neglected the weightier matters of the law: justice and mercy and faithfulness. These you ought to have done, without neglecting the others. You blind guides, straining out a gnat and swallowing a camel!"
> (Matt. 23:23–24)

It's not that tithing mint and dill didn't matter. The Mosaic law required all Hebrews to give a tenth of what they produced for God's work. Mint and dill would have been among the smallest crops. These religious leaders were doing really well in looking after the small things.

The problem, according to Jesus, is that they neglected the weightier matters: justice, mercy, and faithfulness. It's easy to focus on minutiae and overlook the whole point.

It's possible to be a fastidious Christian who attends church, reads the Bible, prays, and cares for their body, but misses out on what matters most to God.

It's possible to be a fastidious Christian who attends church, reads the Bible, prays, and cares for their body, but misses out on what matters most to God.

WHAT MATTERS MOST?

We're going to delve into ways to simplify our spiritual lives. Today, I simply want to raise the issue.

At this point you're practicing six habits, but the habits aren't what matters most. They are means to an end. The habits are meant to bring us closer to God.

Author and theologian D. A. Carson warns:

> The very expression is potentially misleading: spiritual *discipline*, as if there is something intrinsic to self-control, to the imposition of self-discipline, that qualifies one to be more spiritual. Such assumptions and mental associations can lead only to arrogance; worse, they often lead to condescending judgmentalism: others may not be as spiritual as I am since I am *disciplined* enough to have an excellent prayer time or a superb Bible-reading scheme. But the truly transformative element is not the discipline itself, but the worthiness of the task undertaken: the value of prayer, the value of reading God's Word.[1]

This book should have a warning label: *Practicing habits is good, but side effects can include pride and completely missing the point.* The habits are good, but the habits aren't the point. The point is that we were made to know and worship God.

I love how Eric Nels Ortlund puts it: "When I treat daily Bible reading and prayer as something I have to do cause it's good for me (like brushing my teeth), I often don't want to do it. When I open my Bible looking for ways that Jesus is better than I think he is, and thank God for it—it's not a chore any more."[2] Don't just aim to keep habits. Aim to know and love God.

FOR TODAY

Today, simply refocus on what's most important. As you practice your habits, remind yourself that the habits aren't the point. The habits are a means to finding our happiness in God, rather than an end in themselves.

God delights in His children. Draw near to Him today, and He promises to draw near to you (James 4:8).

Reflect and Respond

REVIEW

- We tend to overcomplicate things.
- Pay attention to God's weightier matters: justice, mercy, and faithfulness.
- The point of habits is to find our happiness in God.
- Refocus on what's most important as you practice your habits.

CONSIDER

How are you doing with practicing your habits?

- Where are you focused on what's most important?
- Where do you need to refocus today?
- Do you need to shrink any habits so that you're more focused on what's most important?

DISCUSS

1. Describe a time when you've been focused on the minors (habits, appearances, etc.) and lost sight of God.
2. What reminds you to focus on justice, mercy, faithfulness, and happiness in God?

One Thing Is Necessary

KEEP SERVING, but don't let your service distract you from Jesus.

Mary and Martha, along with their brother Lazarus, were close friends of Jesus. Jesus seemed to enjoy spending time at their house. Jesus had no home of His own. He had "nowhere to lay his head" (Luke 9:58). But He found rest and refuge at the home of these friends.

One time, though, tensions ran high. Mary and Martha welcomed Jesus into their home. Martha probably sensed that Jesus was tired and needed a good dinner. She set to work cleaning and cooking. Providing hospitality was important in that culture, and it was certainly important when Jesus came to visit. Jesus once rebuked another host for not offering Him proper hospitality (Luke 7:36–50).

Martha's sister Mary didn't seem to help. She sat and listened to Jesus' teaching. Predictably, Martha complained. She was "distracted with much serving" (Luke 10:40).

"Martha, Martha," Jesus said, "you are anxious and troubled about many things, but one thing is necessary. Mary has chosen the good portion, which will not be taken away from her." (vv. 41–42)

Martha wasn't wrong to serve Jesus. She was wrong when her service distracted her from the One she served.

THE VALUE OF SERVICE

Some people think that this story tells us to value contemplation over service. That's not what Jesus is telling us. Right before this incident, Jesus told the story of a Samaritan who gave first aid to a victim of a robbery, paid for three weeks of food, and promised to pay the rest of his bills. Jesus finished the story by telling us to be that kind of neighbor to others (Luke 10:37). We need both contemplation *and* service.

When we follow Jesus, we're called into service. If we're not careful, though, our service will distract us from Jesus Himself.

THE DANGER OF DISTRACTIONS

Life is all-consuming. There are always emails to answer, dishes to clean, and bills to be paid. It's never done.

Sometimes, though, it's time to leave the emails unanswered and the dishes unwashed so we can focus on what matters most.

Don't wait until you have time to learn from Jesus. Do it even when you don't have time and even when you're distracted. It's the one thing that's really necessary.

We live in a distracted age, overflowing with entertainment, information, emails, and notifications. Our technology is always on, and we're always connected. "As humans become more stressed, numbed, disoriented, distracted, and paralyzed by the impenetrable glut of information, chaos reigns. As chaos reigns, sin thrives," writes Brett McCracken.[3]

Don't settle for a distracted life. Take steps to keep your focus on what matters most—especially on Jesus.

OVER TO YOU

Look for ways to simplify your habits, to do a little less today, even if it's just a little bit less, so that you have a little more space to focus on Jesus. Seek joy in Him as you:

- Make time for these lessons and habits
- Rest—for a short time daily and a full (or partial) day weekly
- Read or listen to the Bible
- Pray
- Pursue worship and community within a church
- Care for your body

Reflect and Respond

REVIEW

- When we follow Jesus, we're called to serve.
- We need to serve *and* spend time with Jesus.
- Make time for Jesus in the midst of everyday life and distractions.
- Simplify. Do a little less to focus more on Jesus.

CONSIDER

When do you lose your connection with and focus on Jesus?

It is not an "accident" that we move away from what matters most. It's often a byproduct of routines and habits that we are *unaware* of. Next time you catch yourself needing to refocus on Jesus, try reconstructing what happened to find where the connection was lost.

Ask the Holy Spirit to reveal what is needed, and do His work in you to bring your thoughts, behaviors, habits, and rhythms into wholeheartedness in Jesus.

DISCUSS

1. What tends to distract you from what matters most?
2. How can you keep your focus on Jesus?
3. How will you simplify a habit practice, even just a little, to keep your focus on Jesus today?

Declutter

GET RID OF THE CLUTTER that affects your spiritual life.

Char and I have done a couple of kitchen makeovers in our time. We believe that our physical and social environment affects our choices. *If it's in our kitchen, we'll eventually eat it.* To make good food choices, we need to keep healthy, nutritious food in our kitchen and limit or eliminate less nutritious foods that we have acquired over time.

The same thing applies to our spiritual lives. Our spiritual lives aren't just a product of our devotional times. They're the product of lots of other choices that we make. It sounds strange, but that's why it's important to clean out the clutter that affects your spiritual life.

WHAT'S MY CLUTTER?

Getting rid of the clutter means getting rid of the things in your life that interfere with your spiritual growth.

I've found it helpful to think in three categories:

- **Red light actions** are thoughts and behaviors that are just bad news for you. They could be sinful behaviors or patterns that are inconsistent with God's design.

- **Yellow light actions** are thoughts and behaviors that are not necessarily sinful in themselves, but they move you toward sin. You know that if you do them, they will likely lead to red light actions. Or they just impair your ability to engage in green light actions.

- **Green light actions** are healthy, God-honoring choices for you to prioritize. They lead to spiritual thriving, and to less bandwidth or desire for yellow and red light actions.

RED LIGHT

Stop

SINFUL BEHAVIORS AND PATTERNS

"Now the works of the flesh are obvious: sexual immorality, moral impurity, promiscuity, idolatry, sorcery, hatreds, strife, jealousy, outbursts of anger, selfish ambitions, dissensions, factions, envy, drunkenness, carousing, and anything similar." (Gal. 5:19–21 csb)

YELLOW LIGHT

Proceed with Caution

NEUTRAL; MAY MOVE YOU TO SIN OR KEEP YOU FROM GREEN LIGHT ACTIONS

Mindless entertainment
Social media
Excessive recreation
Overwork
Overrest
Situations that expose you to temptation

GREEN LIGHT

Go

PROMOTES GODLINESS AND GROWTH

Reading Scripture   Prayer
Worship   Rest
Fellowship with believers Work
Good food   Reading
Time with friends and family   Exercise

Susanna Wesley, who raised two famous preachers (John and Charles) a few hundred years ago, taught her children how to identify red light behaviors: "whatever weakens your reason, impairs the tenderness of your conscience, obscures your sense of God, or takes off the relish of spiritual things;—in short, whatever increases the strength and authority of your body over your mind, that thing is sin to you, however innocent it may be in itself."[4] For her, sin was anything that lessens our love of God.

If you are struggling with patterns of red light actions—and most of us probably are—then I encourage you to reach out to a pastor, friend, or coach for help. We typically struggle alone, which only makes the struggle harder. Not everyone should know about your struggles, but someone should. Find someone safe who loves God and who will remind you of God's grace. Be courageous, and share honestly about what's going on in your life so you can receive the freedom that Jesus has made possible for you.

It's also important to notice yellow light actions and to begin to get rid of the clutter in this area. For example:

- Are you getting the rest you need to be able to practice your core habits? It's hard to read Scripture, pray, or worship when you're overtired.
- Do you have a time and a place that works for you to practice core habits?
- Are there any activities that tend to crowd out the time you need to practice your core habits?
- Are there any distractions that you can eliminate that would make it easier for you to focus on your habits?

Finally, notice some green light actions that you can take, and do more of them. Are there activities that you know help you connect with God? How can you do more of them?

One caution regarding green light actions: Even good actions can become bad if we're not careful. "The human heart takes good things like a successful career, love, material possessions, even family, and turns them into ultimate things," writes Tim Keller. "Our hearts deify them as the center of our lives, because, we think, they can give us significance and security, safety and fulfillment, if we attain them."[5] Satan likes to weaponize even good things against us. Enjoy God's good gifts and keep taking good actions, but keep them in their rightful place.

FOR TODAY

It's easy to get overwhelmed as we look at all the clutter. For today, just focus on one item from each of the lists:

- What red light action should I eliminate?
- What yellow light action should I minimize?
- What green light action should I increase?

Ask God for His help in answering these questions. Spend a few minutes thinking about the most strategic thing you can do in each of these areas. Make a realistic plan, and then ask for the Holy Spirit's help to follow through.

Reflect and Respond

REVIEW

Our spiritual life is the product of all our choices, not just our spiritual habits.

It's important to get rid of the "clutter"—the thoughts, behaviors, and actions that interfere with our spiritual growth:

- Red light actions—sinful patterns or choices that are inconsistent with God's design
- Yellow light actions—not necessarily sinful but they lead to red light actions or inhibit green light actions
- Green light actions—healthy, God-honoring choices for spiritual thriving

CONSIDER

To increase green light actions, try an experiment with choosing consistency over perfection. We all have days, weeks, or seasons that demand more of us. That's why it's helpful to find ways to simplify our green light habits, to do less than our ideal, so that we experience enjoyment in God in all of our days. A practical way to do this is to create habit "minimums."

For example, if I don't have capacity for my desired prayer time, I will extend my prayer before each of my meals to include worship of God and my needs for the coming hours of the day.

Habit minimums allow us to do what we can with what we have. Minimums allow us to grow in consistency. They help us choose green light actions over yellow and red light actions.

DISCUSS

1. What can you do to deal with red light actions in your life?
2. What is a yellow light action you can minimize?
3. What is a green light action you can increase?
4. What habit minimums can you set to keep your focus on Jesus?

HABIT 7, LESSON 4

What's Slowing You Down?

GET RID OF SOMETHING in your life that's slowing you down.

Therefore, since we are surrounded by so great a cloud of witnesses, let us also lay aside every weight, and sin which clings so closely, and let us run with endurance the race that is set before us, looking to Jesus, the founder and perfecter of our faith, who for the joy that was set before him endured the cross, despising the shame, and is seated at the right hand of the throne of God. (Heb. 12:1–2)

The Christian life is like a race, according to the Bible. Those who have completed the race before us are like spectators watching us. We're in the arena, and all eyes are on us.

Our job? To run. Not to stroll or walk, but to run. Not only that, but to run with endurance. The Christian life is a marathon, not a sprint. Our call is not to coast, but to run with passion, zeal, energy, and discipline.

Our job, besides to run with endurance, is to "lay aside every weight, and sin which clings so closely." The author mentions two categories of needless weight that will slow us down:

- sin (no surprise here)
- other things that aren't sinful, but that will weigh us down as we run

It's not just enough to get rid of things that are wrong. "Nothing which adds weight is retained," comments Donald Guthrie, "all but the bare essentials must be laid aside."[6]

Greek runners would remove their clothes so that they could run unhindered. Talk about a serious commitment to winning!

When I've participated in winter races, I've seen people toss aside blankets and coats at the start of the race. They needed them to keep warm before the race, but once the race starts, they're no longer necessary. Even the best runner will struggle to win the race when carrying excess baggage.

In his book, *Shoe Dog*, Nike founder Phil Knight writes of his business partner Bill Bowerman and his obsession with creating a lighter shoe. A lighter shoe, he explains, translates to greater speed and faster times. Knight explains:

> One ounce sliced off a pair of shoes, he said, is equivalent to 55 pounds over one mile. He wasn't kidding. His math was solid. You take the average man's stride of six feet, spread it out over a mile (5,280 feet), you get 880 steps. Remove one ounce from each step—that's 55 pounds on the button. Lightness, Bowerman believed, directly translated to less burden, which meant more energy, which meant more speed. And speed equaled winning. Bowerman didn't like to lose. (I got it from him.) Thus lightness was his constant goal.[7]

Laying aside every weight—not just pounds but ounces—really matters, in actual races and in the race of faith. Hebrews instructs us to get rid of anything that slows you down.

YOU'RE AN ATHLETE

Following Jesus is like a race, and we're like athletes. Being an athlete is hard work.

Right now you're practicing habits that will help you run the race. It's important to keep practicing these habits, just like athletes train almost every day to stay in shape.

Keep practicing because the race requires endurance. Almost anyone can run for a short distance, but it takes training to go the distance.

In the next habit, we'll look at how to continue to build habits so that you're able to run over the long haul.

As you run this race, remember that the eyes of those who have completed the race are on you. Keep looking to Jesus for the encouragement you need to keep running the race when it's hard. Keep training, and keep running.

You are an athlete, and you're running the race of your life.

TOSS SOMETHING ASIDE

I want to encourage you. You're reading this lesson, which means that you're still tracking with 8 Habits for Growth. Way to go!

Here's another strategy to help you keep going.

Bob Goff, author of *Dream Big*, makes it a practice to regularly quit things:

> Once a year I spread everything out and ask myself, *What do I need to carry with me and what do I need to let go of?* I think

about all the little decisions I make, especially the ones I make regularly, and ask whether all those decisions are working out for me. Are they serving my ambitions or getting in the way?[8]

He also does a smaller version of this every week. Every Thursday, he quits something. "Try this practice for a couple of weeks," he writes. "It will blow your mind."[9]

WHAT TO DO TODAY

Give that strategy a try. Right now, think of one thing that's slowing you down in this race. What's one thing you could toss aside today that would help you run the race better? Quit it so that you can run the race before you.

Reflect and Respond

REVIEW

- The Christian life is like a race.
- We are the athletes.
- Our job is to run with endurance and to simplify, to get rid of sin and anything else that slows us down.

CONSIDER

Take a five-minute life scan.

- What roles (work, volunteer, and personal) are you filling?
- Who are you caring for?
- Where are you spending your time?
- Where are you spending your money?
- What priorities are you pursuing?
- What thoughts and desires drive your behaviors?
- What worries or anxieties are you carrying?

Highlight and celebrate the people, roles, resources, and anything else that is part of your race—your God-given calling and responsibilities.

Review what remains:

- What thoughts or behaviors no longer help you run well?
- Where might you be overdoing it?
- What can you quit?

DISCUSS

1. How are you doing in the race right now?
   - I've got a good pace, running strong
   - A little tired, need a boost
   - Struggling, down, discouraged
   - Other
2. What's one thing in your life that you can toss aside so that you can run better?
3. Who or what could help you succeed in tossing this aside?

Planning for Growth

LEARN SOME PRACTICAL TIPS for staying on track.

You've worked hard to build and practice your habits. As you near the end of this book, plan to make these habits a regular part of your life.

This means moving into maintenance mode. How can we maintain our habits so that we continue to grow spiritually?

Here's a simple plan.

KEEP PRACTICING SMALL, CONSISTENT HABITS

The best way to continue to grow is to keep building small, consistent habits. We don't grow by making massive changes in our lives. We grow by repeatedly practicing small actions that, over time, add up to big changes in our lives.

The good news: spiritual growth is not complex. Dane Ortlund is right: "Read your Bible today. Pray. Love those you come across. It's not complicated folks."[10]

A great way to grow spiritually is to keep it simple. Stick to repeating the basics over a long period of time.

TWO KEYS

1) Progress, not perfection. Still longing to practice your habits perfectly? Good news! That day is coming. On that day, by the grace of God and the work done by Christ, we will experience the mind-blowing, incredible awesomeness of living in perfection. But that day is not now. In this life, progress (not perfection) is the better aim. Progress allows us to move forward with imperfect steps. Progress permits us to fall down, wipe the slate clean, get up, and try again.

> **We grow by repeatedly practicing small actions that, over time, add up to big changes in our lives.**

2) Smaller habits consistently over exceptional habits occasionally. It's the story of the tortoise and the hare. When we have unhealthy aspirations, when we expect exceptional practices and impressive results, we overcommit, run fast, and collapse. As we fall behind, the door is opened to discouragement and self-loathing and we turn to distractions to relieve the pain of failing. When we have healthy aspirations, when we acknowledge even the smallest habits that we are doing by God's grace, we are able to take the next step and do a little more, a little better. We may even do the exceptional in moderation, but our pace is sustainable and we keep on going toward the finish line.

Sometimes we discount the ordinary because we think God only works through extraordinary means. Habits like Bible reading, prayer, community, rest, caring for your body, and simplifying often seem quite ordinary, but they are exactly what God uses to shape us. God uses small, everyday things like these to help us grow.

KEEP THE END IN SIGHT

As we keep practicing these small, consistent habits, let's remember that they're not an end in themselves. They are a means to an end. That end is God.

The purpose of these habits is ultimately to shape our longings and desires so that God becomes our greatest joy and goal. Jesus said, "But seek first the kingdom of God and his righteousness, and all these things will be added to you" (Matt. 6:33).

As you continue to practice your small, consistent habits, ask God to change your heart so that you desire Him above all.

TODAY AND BEYOND

In the final habit, we'll explore some more ways to continue to grow once you're done working through this book.

For today: think about a plan for continuing to practice your habits, and for keeping the end in sight. The habits aren't the end; they're a means to an end. The end is that our hearts long for and become more attentive to God.

Keep going. Keep it simple. Keep practicing your habits. You'll look back and see real growth in your life.

Reflect and Respond

REVIEW

- Plan to keep growing
- Keep practicing small, consistent habits
- Keep the end in sight: that God becomes our greatest joy and goal

Two keys to growth:

1. Pursue progress, not perfection. Don't get discouraged when you fail. Just keep going.
2. Choose smaller habits consistently over exceptional habits occasionally.

CONSIDER

- Where have you seen progress in practicing small, consistent habits? What will you do to celebrate your progress?
- What will help you to keep the goal of enjoying God in sight?

DISCUSS

1. "Progress, not perfection." What is challenging about this? How is this helpful as you plan for the future?
2. "Smaller habits consistently over exceptional habits occasionally." What is challenging about this? How is this helpful as you plan for the future?
3. "Keep the end in sight"—that God becomes our greatest joy. What is challenging about this? How is this helpful as you plan for the future?
4. What is your plan for continuing to practice your habits after you complete *8 Habits for Growth*?
5. Who or what do you need to help your plan succeed?

HABIT #7: SIMPLIFY AND PRIORITIZE

Review

IN THIS HABIT, we've looked at simplifying our spiritual lives. The purpose isn't simplification for its own sake. We simplify so that we can focus on what matters most in our lives.

Here's what we covered:

- Simplify to keep your focus on the main thing.
- Deal with distractions to love and serve well.
- Get rid of clutter by thinking about red light actions to eliminate, yellow light actions to minimize, and green light actions to increase.
- Lay aside something that's slowing you down.
- Plan for future growth.

RESOURCES

Visit gospelforlife.com/simplify for resources on this habit.

CONSIDER

Think about this habit (Simplify and Prioritize).

- What has God revealed to you about Himself?
- How has doing less increased your happiness in God's love and grace for you?
- What went well for you?
- Where did you succeed, even a little bit?
- What can you celebrate?

WHAT TO DO TODAY

Simplify. Take a small action to do a little less in order to keep your focus on pursuing happiness in God.

Then, keep it simple and do what you can to:

- Make time for your habit practices in the coming week
- Rest for a brief time each day and work toward a full day of Sabbath rest once a week
- Engage the Bible
- Speak to God
- Worship and belong
- Care for your body

Group Discussion Questions

READ LUKE 10:38–42.

1. Martha understandably wanted to serve Jesus, but her service caused her to be distracted from what matters most. How do you see this happening in your life?

2. Jesus said, "One thing is necessary." What steps can we take to prevent ourselves from being distracted from the one thing that really matters (learning from Jesus)?

3. What are some examples of things that we could quit so that we are less distracted and more focused on what matters most?

4. What are some approaches to simplifying that you've found effective?

5. What questions do you have about this habit?

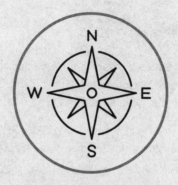

Go the Distance

HABIT

Begin to build a Rule of Life, a set of rhythms and relationships that fit your life.

ASPIRATION

To maintain habits that allow you to continue to grow into Christ-likeness in every area of your life.

CHOOSE YOUR ACTIONS

Choose one or more of the following:

- Make a list of habits you've enjoyed and that have helped you from this book.
- Make a list of key habits that could make a big difference in your life.
- Think about some areas that are working for you, and how you can do more of that.
- Set a timer for ten minutes and work on your Rule of Life.

HABIT 8, LESSON 1

Introducing Habit #8:
Go the Distance

BUILD A SET OF PRACTICES that will provide direction and help you grow.

The habits in this book are designed to help you make lasting changes to your behavior. The first habit is meant to help you prepare for change. Habits 2 through 6 are designed to help you build key behaviors into your life, including the three core habits of the Christian life. The final two habits, including this one, are designed to help you prepare to maintain these behaviors for the rest of your life, and to get back on track when needed. Going the distance requires that you build a plan for continuing to practice these habits, and tweak this plan to fit the circumstances of your life. To do this, I suggest that you build a Rule of Life, almost like an owner's manual for building and continuing these habits.

WHAT'S A RULE OF LIFE?

Some things grow automatically, like weeds and chaos. Almost everything else thrives as a result of feeding, care, and intentionality. This applies to every area of life. You're unlikely to grow in the transformation that God intends for you without thoughtful, intentional choices and deliberate action.

That's where a Rule of Life comes in. A Rule of Life is a set of practices that provide direction and growth. It answers questions like:

- What practices and rhythms are most important?
- How can I order my entire life around God and live with a sense of His presence?
- What do I need to focus on, right now, in order to grow and live fully as God desires?
- When and how should I practice my habits?

Ken Shigematsu writes, "A rule of life is simply a rhythm of practices that empowers us to live well and grow more like Jesus by helping us experience God in everything."[1]

Stephen Macchia defines it as "a holistic description of the Spirit-empowered rhythms and relationships that create, redeem, sustain and transform the life God invites you to humbly fulfill for Christ's glory."[2]

Rule doesn't refer to a set of laws. It's from the Latin word *regula*, which means something done regularly. A Rule of Life is a set of rhythms and relationships that move you toward Christlikeness in every area of life.

BUILD ON THE BASICS

The habits we've covered so far provide a good foundation for growing as God intends, for holy transformation. No matter who we are, how much or little we've grown, we need the basics:

- to make time (for God's transformation in our everyday life)
- to both work and rest
- to read or listen to God's Word
- to pray
- to pursue worship and a community of healthy relationships with followers of Jesus Christ
- to care for our bodies
- to simplify and prioritize so that we're focusing on what matters most

As you move beyond this book, you will want to continue to practice these habits in sustainable ways. Building a Rule of Life bridges the gap between desire and reality.

WHAT TO DO TODAY

In the coming lessons, I'll give you some guidelines on developing your own Rule of Life. For today, begin to reflect on these questions.

- What habits have you particularly enjoyed from this book? Why do you think you enjoyed them so much?
- What habits did you struggle with? Why do you think you struggled with them?
- Where do you sense God is calling you to stretch and grow right now?
- What core habits, practiced regularly, would make a big difference in your life?

Answering these questions will help you begin to build a Rule of Life that's most helpful for you.

Reflect and Respond

REVIEW

A Rule of Life is a set of rhythms, practices, and relationships that allow you to live well, become more like Jesus, and experience God in every area of life.

It answers questions like:

- What practices and rhythms are most important?
- How can I order my entire life around God and live with a sense of His presence?
- What do I need to focus on, right now, in order to grow and live fully as God desires?
- When and how should I practice my habits?

It allows you to build on the basic habits of:

- making time
- resting
- reading or listening to the Bible
- praying
- pursuing worship and community in a church
- caring for your body
- simplifying and prioritizing

CONSIDER

- **How is your heart?** Have you slipped into performing habits in your own strength? Are your habits drawing you closer to God?
- **Where is the Holy Spirit at work?** Are you relying on your own motivation or asking the Holy Spirit for help? What has the Holy Spirit done in you that you could not do on your own?
- **What is God revealing to you?** What truths encourage or challenge you? What are you learning about yourself? About God? Where do you sense God calling you to stretch and grow?

DISCUSS

1. What habits have you enjoyed? Choose as many as you like.
2. What did you enjoy about these habits?
3. What habits have you struggled with? Choose as many as you like.
4. What was hard for you with these habits? Be as specific as possible.
5. What small step will you take today to experience God's presence in your life?

HABIT 8, LESSON 2

Build On What's Working

NOTICE WHAT'S WORKING, and do more of that.

Chip and Dan Heath, authors of *Switch: How to Change When Change Is Hard*, describe a challenge that many of us face. We tend to focus on the negative. When things go well, we don't always notice. When things break, we snap to attention and try to fix them.

Imagine a world in which you experienced a rush of gratitude every single time you flipped a light switch and the room lit up. Imagine a world in which after a husband forgot his wife's birthday, she gave him a big kiss and said, "For thirteen of the last fourteen years you remembered my birthday! That's wonderful!"[3]

This is not our world.

The Heath brothers suggest a simple question to help us shift the focus to a more positive focus: "What's working, and how can we do more of it?"[4] It's a great question to ask in every area of life. It will also help us build our Rule of Life.

WHAT'S WORKING?

You've spent time working through this book. I'm sure that you've found that some habits have worked for you, and some haven't. It's a good idea to take a step back and ask, "What's working?"

- **Make time**—What's helped you to make the time to work through this book and build new habits?
- **Rest**—Have you found a way to rest that works for you?
- **Read or listen to the Bible**—Is there a way that you've read or listened to the Bible that has been particularly effective?
- **Pray**—What helps you pray for at least five minutes a day?
- **Get involved with a church**—What practices help you prepare for worship and experience community?
- **Care for your body**—What helps you to move, eat tasty, nutritious food slowly, or get a little more rest or sleep?
- **Simplify and prioritize**—What helps you clear distractions and get rid of clutter so you're focused on what matters most?

Rather than focus on the negative, shine the spotlight on what's worked. Look for what's worked, and do more of that.

BUILDING YOUR RULE OF LIFE

A Rule of Life is a set of rhythms and relationships to help you grow spiritually. It's customized for you. While we're all called to do certain things (read or listen to the Bible, pray, and worship, for instance), we'll all do these in different ways depending on our personalities and the demands on our lives.

Some of us thrive on introspection and silence. Some of us are fueled by spending time with others. Some of us function best in the morning, while some of us do better at night.

Some of us have flexible schedules. Others are in a season of busyness and don't have as much flexibility.

While it's important to stretch ourselves, it's also important to begin with a solid understanding of how we work best, and to begin to build our own Rule of Life on what works for us in this season.

WHAT TO DO TODAY

Notice what works

Enjoy an unstructured approach? After you practice a habit, simply ask, "How's that working for me?"

Enjoy a structured approach to uncover what is working for you? Put on your scientist hat after you practice a habit. Then:

1. **Rate your habit practice** between 0 to 10, where 0 is "This is life-sucking; I do not sense God's presence," and 10 is "This is life-giving and increases my awareness of God's presence." You're not judging performance. The rating reflects whether you are moving toward your why and how well your practice lines up with how God has made you.
2. **Capture the details.** What exactly are you doing as you practice this habit? Where are you? What time of day is it? Who is with you? What is motivating you?
3. **Notice and name connections.** What practices, people, times of day, and places are life-giving and nourish your relationship with God? What practices, people, times of day, and places move you away from your relationship with God?
4. **Adapt, adjust, repeat, and look for changes, no matter how small.** What works even a little? What can you do to do a little more a little better?

In the next lesson, we'll look at how to build a Rule of Life. For now, focus on noticing what's working for you, build on what's working, and celebrate your successes.

Reflect and Respond

REVIEW

Shift to a positive focus: What's working? How can I do more of that? What helps me succeed with these habits?

- **Make Time**
- **Rest and Refresh**
- **Engage the Bible**
- **Speak with God**
- **Worship and Belong**
- **Care for Your Body**
- **Simplify and Prioritize**

CONSIDER

- How's your pursuit of happiness in God going? Where are you experiencing greater joy, delight, and satisfaction in God?
- What practices increase your sense of wholeheartedness: living out of your core, being known and loved by God?
- When are you reminded that you are known and loved by God through what Jesus has done?

DISCUSS

Keep building the foundation for your Rule of Life.

1. What habits work really well for you?
2. What bright spots do you see in the habits that work well for you?
3. How can you build on these bright spots as you develop your Rule of Life?
4. What action will you take today to build on a bright spot as you practice your habits?

HABIT 8, LESSON 3

How to Build a Rule of Life

PREPARE TO BEGIN writing your Rule of Life.

When we encounter difficult or unexpected situations, we often find ourselves problem-solving instead of purpose-finding. I read this story of a dad introducing the idea of making a "Life Statement" to his daughter who was in a moment like that.

The father "explained that it is a short document in which I try to capture the essence of who I am and what my purpose is in life."

"You have an actual document that does that?" his daughter asked.

The father said, "Let me show you my life statement." He recounts what happened next:

She followed me into my study. I reached into a file, pulled out a sheet of paper, and handed it to her. . . .

[She] read the document carefully and then looked up. . . . She asked, "When you feel bad, you read this and it makes you feel better?"

"No, when I feel really bad, I take my life statement out, read it carefully, and try to rewrite any part of it that I feel needs revision. Or I add something that was not there before. The document is always evolving. When I finish rewriting it, I feel clearer about who I am."

She spent the weekend writing a first draft of her own statement. By the time she returned home, she felt "happier, more confident and ready to move forward."[5]

BUILDING YOUR RULE OF LIFE

We need clarity about what matters most and what we need to do to keep our focus on our greatest priorities. Shari's father calls this a life statement. I prefer to call it a Rule of Life.

A Rule of Life is a set of rhythms, practices, and relationships that allow you to live well, become more like Jesus, and experience God in every area of life. It clarifies what matters most, and helps you become more intentional and less reactive in how you live.

Building a Rule of Life is highly personal. It involves thinking carefully about the practices and rhythms that work best for you. Your Rule of Life will have some similarities to others, but it will also be unique to you.

You can benefit immediately from writing a Rule of Life because it helps to clarify what matters most to you. But it's also a living document that may change over time. The benefits will increase as you update it when you gain clarity or face different demands.

It's best to start simple and just get going. Shrink the challenge. Don't expect to write a masterpiece. Jot a few thoughts or sentences down and return to it later.

HOW TO WRITE A RULE OF LIFE

Developing a Rule of Life doesn't have to be complicated.

"My most important counsel is to start small and simply," advises Ken Shigematsu. He suggests that you start with one practice at a time, beginning with a practice that connects you to God. When ready, he says, add a practice that brings refreshment, followed by a practice that connects you to others through relationship and service.[6]

"A sustainable rule of life will be built slowly, tested, and regularly revised," he writes. It must honor our personality, design, and stage of life. "We don't exist for the rule. The rule exists for us."[7]

Here are three simple steps you can take as you begin to build your Rule of Life.

1. **List your categories.** Keep it simple. What are the main areas of your life? Examples: spiritual, physical, relational, vocational. (Although it's helpful to think in categories, they're interrelated and interdependent. As you work on each category, think also of your life as a whole.)

2. **Pick one.** Pick one category, and think about one practice that will help you thrive and grow in that area. Focus on a practice that helps you become aware of God's presence and love, provides the greatest nourishment, refreshment, and renewal, and helps you love others. What's the practice? Why is it important to you?

3. **Think about what works for you.** How often will you do this practice? Realistically, when will you do it? How can you start a new habit so that you're confident that you can do it consistently?

That's it. Start small with only one action or habit, and return to it later. Repeat this process for a short amount of time each day, and you'll begin to build an effective Rule of Life.

WHAT TO DO TODAY

Set a timer for ten minutes, and go through the steps described above. At the end of the ten minutes, continue if you'd like, or stop. No pressure. You can return to it later.

Warning: some people get stuck here. Treat this as a messy first draft. Keep it as short as you'd like. Don't worry about getting it perfect. Just get it started, and you can edit it over time.

Then do what you can to practice each of your habits.

Building a Rule of Life

Choose your categories. Examples: • spiritual, physical, relational, vocational • devotions, work, family, church, body • health, work, relationships, recreation	**My Categories:**
Pick a category. Example: "Right now, I want to focus on my spiritual life."	**Right now I would like to focus on the following category:**
Select a practice. Example: "I want to read the Bible."	**Out of all the practices I could choose in this category, the one that is most strategic for me right now is:**
Think about what works for you. Make the practice small and specific. Shrink the practice until you're confident you can perform this action consistently. Example: "I will find a Bible reading plan. Every morning, I will read the Bible using that plan for 20 minutes when I wake up."	**My small, specific plan is:**

Rule of Life Worksheet

Questions for Each Category

1. What's worked for you in this category already? How can you do more of that?
2. What practices would help you become aware of God's presence and love, provide the greatest nourishment, refreshment, and renewal, and help you love others?
3. How often will you do it? When?
4. Are you confident that you can do the practices consistently? If not, shrink them until you are.

See the appendix ("Sample Practices").

SPIRITUAL

Practices

1. _____

Specific Plan (what, when, where): _____
_____
_____
_____

2. _____

Specific Plan (what, when, where): _____
_____
_____
_____

3. _____

Specific Plan (what, when, where): _____
_____
_____
_____

PHYSICAL

Practices

1. _____

Specific Plan (what, when, where): _____
_____
_____
_____

2. _____

Specific Plan (what, when, where): _____
_____
_____
_____

3. _____

Specific Plan (what, when, where): _____
_____
_____
_____

RELATIONAL

Practices

1. _____

Specific Plan (what, when, where): _____
_____
_____
_____

2. _____

Specific Plan (what, when, where): _____
_____
_____
_____

3. _____

Specific Plan (what, when, where): _____

_____

_____

_____

VOCATIONAL

Practices

1. _____

Specific Plan (what, when, where): _____

_____

_____

_____

2. _____

Specific Plan (what, when, where): _____

_____

_____

_____

3. _____

Specific Plan (what, when, where): _____

_____

_____

_____

OTHER

Practices

1. _____

Specific Plan (what, when, where): _____

_____

_____

_____

2. _____

Specific Plan (what, when, where): _____

_____

_____

_____

3. _____

Specific Plan (what, when, where): _____

_____

_____

_____

Reflect and Respond

REVIEW

To begin building your Rule of Life:

- List the main categories of your life (e.g., spiritual, physical, relational, vocational, etc.).
- Pick one category, and work on one practice. Focus on practices that help you love God and others.
- Think about what works for you. Think about what will work best in your life. Shrink the challenge until you're confident that you can do it consistently.
- Repeat for a few moments each day as you continue to build your Rule of Life.

CONSIDER

- It doesn't have to be perfect.
- Keep it simple.
- Have fun.

ACTION

Set the timer for ten minutes again today to keep working on your Rule of Life. When ten minutes is over, you can choose to continue or to stop until another day. No pressure.

HABIT 8, LESSON 4

Revisit Your Motivation

REVISIT YOUR MOTIVATION, celebrate success, and take the next step.

In Habit 1, Lesson 3, you explored your motivation:

In just a few weeks, if you keep going, you'll have finished this book. You'll have read forty lessons, answered numerous questions, and practiced eight habits. I hope you'll also have enjoyed working through this book alone or, even better, with others.

This isn't a long time, but it's long enough to make meaningful progress. When you finish the last lesson, how do you hope that your life has changed?

For now, don't worry about being practical. Picture the future you. Where do you want to be? How do you want to feel? How will your life have changed? Try to describe your hopes and goals in as much detail as possible.

- I want to be . . .
- I want to feel . . .
- I want to change . . .

It's time for these answers to help you take the next step. Take a moment to review your answers from the first week. Ask yourself the following questions:

- What progress have you made toward these hopes and goals?
- How can you celebrate your progress?
- What habits will help you continue to move toward these goals?
- How can you be sustained and encouraged in this journey?
- What new hopes and goals is God growing in your heart now?

THE INFINITE JOURNEY

The journey we're on will never end in this life. We will never arrive until after the resurrection. One author calls this an infinite journey. The journey of spiritual growth is "the internal journey of an individual Christian from being dead in sin to gloriously perfect in Christ." He reminds us that it's not easy: "The internal journey of individual, personal salvation—from justification, through sanctification, into glorification—is also a gradual process requiring great effort, labor, and suffering."[8]

The good news is that we don't take this journey alone. God has given us others to walk alongside us. Best of all, He's given us the Spirit, who is changing every part of who we are from the inside out. God is completely committed to us until the job is over.

"I am sure of this, that he who began a good work in you will bring it to completion at the day of Jesus Christ." (Phil. 1:6)

Because the journey is an infinite one, we'll always see how far we have to go. It's good to stop, take a look back, and remind ourselves that God is at work in our messy and imperfect lives, and that He's committed to seeing us complete the journey.

KEEP GOING

You're working on building a Rule of Life in this habit. It's a set of practices and rhythms that will help you continue to grow. It doesn't have to be fancy. It should just be something that will help you take the next step in your journey.

Take another ten minutes today for your Rule of Life. Continue this process, ten minutes at a time, in the coming weeks.

Look for small, practical steps you can take to continue the progress you've already made. **Focus on what's gone well** rather than what hasn't. **Add more of the good** rather than focusing on what's missing.

God is committed to your growth. He's committed to you. Keep going!

Reflect and Respond

REVIEW

- The journey to spiritual maturity is slow and gradual; it requires intentional effort, work, and suffering.
- We are not meant to do it alone; we are designed to grow in community with others.
- The Holy Spirit is changing every part of who we are from the inside out.
- God is faithful. He's committed to seeing us complete the journey.

A Rule of Life helps to keep us:

- motivated and sustained
- focused on what's going well
- able to see progress
- celebrating success, even in suffering, as we grow in happiness in God
- adding more of the good to take the next step

CONSIDER

- What helps you to look for the good?
- How do you like to celebrate?
- Where will you add a little more of the good?

DISCUSS

1. As you look back on your goals, what signs of progress can you celebrate?
2. How will you celebrate the work God has done and increase your happiness in God today?
3. As you look forward, what steps can you take to continue the journey?

Using Your Rule of Life

USE YOUR RULE OF LIFE to build habits in your life.

It really doesn't look like much. Making time, resting, reading or listening to the Bible, praying, pursuing worship and community in a church, caring for your body, and simplifying are all important, but they're also humble. Few people will notice if you do them, at least at first. Few people will notice if you stop. Over time, though, practicing these habits leads to big changes.

God works through the ordinary means of grace, through our repeated small acts of faithfulness to Him.

Matt Redmond writes:

But I say, be nobody special. Do your job. Take care of your family. Clean your house. Mow your yard. Read your Bible. Attend worship. Pray. Watch your life and doctrine closely. Love your spouse. Love your kids. Be generous. Laugh with your friends. Drink your wine heartily. Eat your meat lustily. Be honest. Be kind to your waitress. Expect no special treatment. And do it all quietly.

... be faithful right where you are, regardless of how mundane that place is.[9]

And repeat.

Keep going! With God's help, you will continue to change as you pursue habits that shape your heart to love God more. It's the pathway to growth for "taxi-driving, errand-running moms; to hardworking, overcommitted dads; to homework-heavy, extracurricular-busy students; to schedule-packed singles; to responsibility-overloaded single parents—in short, to every believer."[10]

USE YOUR RULE OF LIFE TODAY

Keep working on your Rule of Life for ten minutes today. And continue to work on it, ten minutes at a time, over the next weeks. Revise it whenever you need to make it work better or to refocus on the rhythms and practices that help you love God and others.

Keep practicing your habits from this book. Incorporate them in your Rule of Life. Allow these habits to direct your heart to Jesus. Notice and celebrate times of joy in God. Add more of that!

Practice your habits. Take the next step. God be with you.

Reflect and Respond

REVIEW

- Practicing small, consistent habits leads to big changes.
- Be faithful in ordinary things.
- Use your Rule of Life to grow habits that shape your heart to love God more.
- Keep working on your Rule of Life: start where you are, use what's working.
- Practice your habits: do what you can, notice times of joy in God.
- Take the next step: celebrate what God is doing, add more of the good.

CONSIDER

- What's working right now?
- When does it work? When does it not work?
- What can you do to shrink the challenge when you have less capacity?
- What is bringing you joy in God? How could you add more of that in another area of your life?
- Where is God prompting you to grow?

ACTION

1. What steps will you take to continue to practice habits that lead to growth?
2. What challenges do you anticipate?
3. What, if anything, do you need to help you take the next step?

HABIT #8: GO THE DISTANCE

Review

WE'VE BEEN LOOKING at how to create a Rule of Life: a set of rhythms and relationships to help us grow in every area of life. We've done this by:

- defining a Rule of Life
- finding what's already working so you can do more of that
- beginning to work on your Rule of Life by focusing on one category and one practice
- revisiting your motivation and celebrating success
- using your Rule of Life to build habits that shape your heart

RESOURCES

Visit gospelforlife.com/rule-of-life for resources on this habit.

CONSIDER

Think about building your Rule of Life.

- What's gone well for you so far?
- Where did you succeed, even a little bit?
- What can you celebrate?
- Who will you share your Rule of Life with for encouragement and support?

WHAT TO DO TODAY

Set a timer for ten minutes and keep working on the draft of your Rule of Life. Remember: it doesn't have to be perfect. Treat it like a working document. Keep looking for ways to make these practices work in your life to help you grow in your love for God and others.

Then, do what you can to:

- Make time for your habit practices in the coming week
- Rest for a brief time each day and work toward a full day of Sabbath rest once a week
- Read or listen to the Bible
- Pray
- Pursue worship and community in a church
- Care for your body
- Simplify and prioritize

Group Discussion Questions

READ ECCLESIASTES 12:9–14.

1. The writer of Ecclesiastes explored different approaches to life, and concluded that the whole purpose of life is to fear God and keep His commandments. How does this bring clarity to your life?

2. Ecclesiastes 12:14 reminds us that God will one day evaluate our lives. How does that help to shape the decisions we make right now? What kinds of changes should we make in light of this?

3. This conclusion is meant to bring us joy. "It is not only the beginning of wisdom; it is also the beginning of joy, of contentment and of an energetic and purposeful life. . . . He wishes to drive us to see that God is there, that He is good and generous, and that only such an outlook makes life coherent and fulfilling."[11] How do these verses help you see God's goodness and generosity to you?

4. Why do you think it's so easy to lose track of the main point of life and live for lesser things?

5. What habits and practices from this book have helped you focus on the main point of fearing God and keeping His commandments?

6. How is it going with writing your Rule of Life so far? Where do you need help?

7. Do you have any questions about how to build a Rule of Life?

APPENDIX

Sample Practices

Use the following examples of practices for ideas as you build your own Rule of Life. Choose the ones that help you grow in your love for God and others, and that are sustainable. Tweak the practices so they fit your life, and add your own ideas.

DOMAIN: SPIRITUAL

Habit: Make Time

Sample practices:

- Set a daily appointment for Bible reading and prayer, and put it in my calendar.
- Set an alarm to pray three times a day.

Habit: Engage the Bible

Sample practices:

- Read three chapters of the Bible each day.
- Find and follow a Bible reading plan.
- Read a devotional each night before bed.
- Memorize one verse of Scripture each week.

- Find friends who want to read the Bible regularly, and form a group. Check in every week for discussion and mutual support.
- Implement a "Scripture before phone" policy: read the Bible each day before picking up the phone.

Habit: Speak with God

Sample practices:

- Spend ten minutes in prayer each day.
- Journal my prayers.
- Take a prayer walk once a week.
- Phone a prayer partner once a week.
- Use the PrayerMate app each morning to guide me through my prayer time.
- Create and follow a plan to pray for different categories each day (e.g., family on Monday and Thursday, friends on Tuesday and Friday, and ministries on Wednesday and Saturday).
- Pray with spouse for five minutes each morning.
- Pray a liturgy from *Every Moment Holy*[1] once a week.

Habit: Worship and Belong

Sample practices:

- Regularly attend a small group at church.
- Attend church each Sunday.

Habit: Simplify and Prioritize

Sample practices:

- Take a personal retreat day each quarter for planning.
- Take a social media fast for a month each year.
- Practice a digital fast for one day each week.

- Turn my phone and internet off for one hour each day.
- Dock and silence my smartphone each evening at 6:00.
- Delete social media apps on my phone.
- Use an app to restrict my screen time, outside of work, to one hour a day.
- Turn off notifications.

Habit: Go the Distance

Sample practices:

- Listen to Christian music while commuting.
- Read a book on spiritual disciplines and habits each year.
- Read a classic Christian book each year, like *Knowing God* by J. I. Packer, or *The Pilgrim's Progress* by John Bunyan.
- Tweak my Rule of Life once a month so it fits my life better and helps me to grow in my love for God and others.

DOMAIN: PHYSICAL

Habit: Care for Your Body (with Food)

Sample practices:

- Sign up for a meal kit that allows me to cook healthy food at home.
- Reserve thirty minutes for each meal to allow enough time to eat slowly.
- Shop at the farmer's market for vegetables each week.

Habit: Care for Your Body (with Movement)

Sample practices:

- Take a walk every other day.

- Exercise for thirty minutes three times a week.
- Every month, try one new physical activity that I might enjoy.
- Set an alarm to remind me to get outside and go for a walk each day.

DOMAIN: RELATIONAL

Habit: Worship and Belong

Sample practices:

- Send one note or text of encouragement each week.
- Invite one person to dinner every month.
- Keep a list of "one another" commands and try to practice a new one every month.
- Schedule annual retreat with close friends who know me well, and are committed to walk with me and help me grow in my love for God.
- Take a friend with me when I go grocery shopping so we have an opportunity to grow in our relationship.

Habit: Simplify and Prioritize

Sample practices:

- Take one action each week to build a relationship with a neighbor.
- Schedule a meal with one friend each week.
- Create a phone-free zone at the dinner table.
- Volunteer in the community once a week.
- Schedule weekly date night with spouse.
- Schedule a recurring family night.

DOMAIN: VOCATIONAL

Sample practices:

- Set one major priority for work each day.
- Take one new course each year to develop my skills.
- Meet with a mentor once a month.

DOMAIN: FREE TIME

Habit: Make Time

Sample practices:

- Finish work by 5:00 each workday.
- Create and follow an "Ideal Week" calendar that shows, generally speaking, how I would like to structure my week.[2]

Habit: Rest and Refresh

Sample practices:

- Practice one daily action that brings me rest each day (e.g., taking a nap or bath, going for a walk, reading a book).
- Start a new hobby that brings me joy.
- Take one complete Sabbath day each week.
- Aim to go to bed each night by 10:30.
- Relax in the bath at least once a week.
- Book a half day every month for reflection and planning.
- Read one book a month.
- Create a reading list of books I would love to read, and update it weekly.
- Read for thirty minutes every day.

RECOMMENDED RESOURCES

FOR RECOMMENDED RESOURCES on the habits in this book, and two bonuses ("Using Habits for Growth in Your Church" and "Helping Others Grow"), please visit gospelforlife.com/resources.

ABOUT GOSPEL FOR LIFE

MANY CHRISTIANS FEEL STUCK. They want to grow in their love for God and others, but many have not had someone walk with them and show them how. Churches and pastors serve faithfully, but could use some support in helping their people to grow.

Gospel for Life provides clear, practical, and biblical resources for growth resulting in transformed lives and effective churches. We help churches make disciples.

Please visit gospelforlife.com and follow us at @insideG4L.

ACKNOWLEDGMENTS

CHAR'S DECISION TO LEAVE her accounting work began a cascade of events that led to this book. I'm beyond grateful for her life and how she's shaped what I've written.

Char's father, Ron Hartwick, started asking me about my next book a long time ago. I'm grateful for his encouragement.

Thanks to my brother David Dash, along with his wife Liz, who allowed me to stay at their house for a week, while they were away, to work on this book.

Thanks to the 94 people (and counting) who took G4L Coaching and provided feedback and encouragement on this material.

Jen Pollock Michel is one of my favorite contemporary authors. She helped me recruit some amazing people to go through the first draft of this material, and now she's written the foreword. She's a great writer and a helpful friend.

I'm very grateful for my agent Steve Laube's wisdom and experience, and that he was willing to represent me.

I love working with Moody Publishers. Thanks to Drew Dyck and Connor Sterchi for editing this book, Erik Peterson and Brandi Davis for making it look good, and Melissa Zaldivar and Kathryn Eastham for helping me get the word out.

And thanks to Liberty Grace Church, Toronto, for the privilege of being their pastor.

NOTES

HABIT #1: MAKE TIME

1. "Power of Habit: Q&A with Author Charles Duhigg," Penguin Random House Library Marketing, November 9, 2011, https://penguinrandom-houselibrary.com/2011/11/09/power-of-habit-qa-with-author-charles-duhigg/.
2. BJ Fogg, *Tiny Habits* (Boston: Mariner Books, 2020), 2, Kindle.
3. Nick Needham, *Daily Readings – The Early Church Fathers* (Fearn, Scotland: Christian Focus Publications, 2017), loc. 2306, Kindle.
4. Christopher Love, "Weak Measures of Grace in Christians," http://articles.ochristian.com/article13325.shtml.
5. Jen Pollock Michel, *Teach Us to Want: Longing, Ambition and the Life of Faith* (Downers Grove, IL: InterVarsity Press, 2014), 92, Kindle.
6. Sam Storms, *Pleasures Evermore: The Life-Changing Power of Enjoying God* (Colorado Springs: The Navigators, 2000), 29, 33–34, Kindle.
7. Ibid., 31–32.
8. Ibid., 33.
9. George Müller, *A Narrative of Some of the Lord's Dealings with George Müller*, 3rd ed. (London: J. Nisbet, 1845), 417.
10. Darryl Dash, *How to Grow: Applying the Gospel to All of Your Life* (Chicago: Moody Publishers, 2018), 81.

HABIT #2: REST AND REFRESH

1. Leonard Sweet, *The Well-Played Life: Why Pleasing God Doesn't Have to Be Such Hard Work* (Carol Stream, IL: Tyndale Momentum, 2014), 12–13, Kindle.
2. J. I. Packer, *God's Plans for You* (Wheaton, IL: Crossway, 2001), 84.
3. Reggie McNeal, *A Work of Heart: Understanding How God Shapes Spiritual Leaders* (San Francisco: Jossey-Bass, 2011), 147.

4. Eugene Peterson, *Working the Angles: The Shape of Pastoral Integrity* (Grand Rapids, MI: William B. Eerdmans, 1989), 73.

5. Suzanne Koven, "Busy Is the New Sick," Boston.com, July 31, 2017, http://archive.boston.com/lifestyle/health/blog/inpractice/2013/07/busy_is_the_new_sick.html.

6. Philip Nation, *Habits for Our Holiness: How the Spiritual Disciplines Grow Us Up, Draw Us Together, and Send Us Out* (Chicago: Moody Publishers, 2016), 118.

7. Ryan McGraw, *The Day of Worship: Reassessing the Christian Life in Light of the Sabbath* (Grand Rapids, MI: Reformation Heritage Books, 2011), loc. 1955, Kindle.

8. Christopher Ash, *Zeal without Burnout: Seven Keys to a Lifelong Ministry of Sustainable Sacrifice* (Epsom, England: The Good Book Company, 2016), loc. 466, Kindle.

9. John Piper, "A Brief Theology of Sleep," Desiring God, August 3, 1982, https://www.desiringgod.org/articles/a-brief-theology-of-sleep.

10. A. J. Swoboda, *Subversive Sabbath: The Surprising Power of Rest in a Nonstop World* (Grand Rapids, MI: Baker Publishing Group), loc. 131, Kindle.

11. Marva J. Dawn, *Keeping the Sabbath Wholly* (Grand Rapids, MI: William B. Eerdmans, 2003), 65–66.

12. Matthew Sleeth, *24/6: A Prescription for a Healthier, Happier Life* (Carol Stream, IL: Tyndale, 2012), 102, Kindle.

13. Ibid., 102.

14. Ibid., 25.

15. Justin Huffman, "Is the Sabbath Command Still Relevant?," Justin Huffman.org, June 24, 2020, https://justinhuffman.org/2020/06/24/is-the-sabbath-command-still-relevant/.

16. John Piper, "What Does It Mean Practically to Keep the Sabbath Holy?," Desiring God, December 26, 2008, https://www.desiringgod.org/interviews/what-does-it-mean-practically-to-keep-the-sabbath-holy.

17. Chuck DeGroat, *Wholeheartedness: Busyness, Exhaustion, and Healing the Divided Self* (Grand Rapids, MI: Eerdmans, 2016), 8–9, Kindle.

18. Ibid., 9.

19. George Guthrie, *Hebrews*, The NIV Application Commentary (Grand Rapids, MI: Zondervan Publishing House, 1998), 166.

20. Jamin Goggin and Kyle Strobel, *Beloved Dust: Drawing Close to God by Discovering the Truth about Yourself* (Nashville: Nelson Books, 2014), 161, 171–72, Kindle.

HABIT #3: ENGAGE THE BIBLE

1. Donald S. Whitney, *Spiritual Disciplines for the Christian Life* (Colorado Springs: NavPress, 2014), 28, Kindle.

2. As quoted in *444 Surprising Quotes about the Bible: A Treasury of Inspiring Thoughts and Classic Quotations*, comp. Isabella D. Bunn (Bloomington, MN: Bethany House Publishers, 2005), 13.

3. James Clear, "Vince Lombardi on the Hidden Power of Mastering the Fundamentals," JamesClear.com, https://jamesclear.com/vince-lombardi-fundamentals.

4. Bible League Canada, "Canadian Bible Engagement Study," https://bibleleague.ca/bibleengagementstudy/.

5. George H. Guthrie, *Read the Bible for Life: Your Guide to Understanding and Living God's Word* (Nashville: B&H, 2011), loc. 169–71, Kindle.

6. David Mathis, *Habits of Grace: Enjoying Jesus through the Spiritual Disciplines* (Wheaton, IL: Crossway, 2016), 45, Kindle.

7. Calculations based on word counts from Jeffrey Kranz, "Word Counts for Every Book of the Bible (Free Download)," OverviewBible.com, May 29, 2014, https://overviewbible.com/word-counts-books-of-bible/.

8. https://bibleproject.com/.

9. Mathis, *Habits of Grace*, 54.

10. James Nichols, *Puritan Sermons*, vol. 2 (Wheaton, IL: Richard Owen Roberts, Publishers, 1981), 65.

11. Geoffrey Thomas, *Reading the Bible* (Edinburgh: Banner of Truth, 1981), 22.

12. Ibid.

13. "The Bible in 40 Days," DashHouse, April 28, 2020, https://dashhouse.com/the-bible-in-40-days/.

14. Sally Lloyd-Jones, *The Jesus Storybook Bible: Every Story Whispers His Name* (Grand Rapids, MI: Zondervan, 2007).

HABIT #4: SPEAK WITH GOD

1. Paul E. Miller, *A Praying Life: Connecting with God in a Distracting World* (Colorado Springs: NavPress, 2017), loc. 290, Kindle.

2. Tim Kerr, *22 Life Lessons on Prayer* (self-pub., 2019), 6.

3. Linette Martin, *Practical Praying* (Grand Rapids, MI: Eerdmans, 1997), 21–22.

4. Jared C. Wilson, *The Imperfect Disciple: Grace for People Who Can't Get Their Act Together* (Grand Rapids, MI: Baker Books, 2017), 110, Kindle.

5. Sinclair B. Ferguson, *In Christ Alone: Living the Gospel Centered Life* (Lake Mary, FL: Reformation Trust, 2007), 145, Kindle.

6. Miller, *A Praying Life*, loc. 862.

7. Ibid., loc. 3268.

8. https://www.prayermate.net/app.

9. Douglas Kaine McKelvey and Ned Bustard, *Every Moment Holy* (Nashville: Rabbit Room Press, 2007).

10. Arthur Bennett, *The Valley of Vision* (Edinburgh: Banner of Truth, 2004).

11. Timothy Keller (@timkellernyc), Twitter, March 16, 2018, https://twitter.com/timkellernyc/status/974647483711320065?lang=en.

HABIT #5: WORSHIP AND BELONG

1. John R. W. Stott, *God's New Society: The Message of Ephesians*, The Bible Speaks Today (Downers Grove, IL: InterVarsity Press, 1979), 129.

2. C. Michael Patton, *Now That I'm a Christian: What It Means to Follow Jesus* (Wheaton, IL: Crossway, 2014), loc. 1391, Kindle.

3. Tim Chester and Steve Timmis, *Total Church: A Radical Reshaping around Gospel and Community* (Wheaton, IL: Crossway, 2008), 50.

4. Ibid.

5. Ray Ortlund, "How to Build a Gospel Culture in Your Church," The Gospel Coalition, Orlando 2015, https://media.thegospelcoalition.org/static-blogs/ray-ortlund/files/2015/07/Paper.pdf.

6. Gavin Ortlund's book *Finding the Right Hills to Die On: The Case for Theological Triage* (Wheaton, IL: Crossway, 2020) is helpful in discerning which theological issues matter most.

7. Megan Hill, "Your Seat in Church Is a Seat in Heaven," https://www.thegospelcoalition.org/article/church-seat-heaven/.

8. David Mathis, *Habits of Grace: Enjoying Jesus through the Spiritual Disciplines* (Wheaton, IL: Crossway, 2016), 156–57, Kindle.

9. Donald S. Whitney, *Spiritual Disciplines for the Christian Life* (Colorado Springs: NavPress, 2014), 111, Kindle.

10. Jake Belder (@jakebelder), Twitter, September 25, 2016, https://twitter.com/jakebelder/status/780146937911713792.

11. Mike Cosper, *Rhythms of Grace: How the Church's Worship Tells the Story of the Gospel* (Wheaton, IL: Crossway, 2013), loc. 1515, Kindle.

12. Larry Crabb, *Becoming a True Spiritual Community: A Profound Vision of What the Church Can Be* (Nashville: Thomas Nelson, 1999), loc. 533, Kindle.

13. Tony Payne, *How to Walk into Church* (Youngstown, OH: Matthias Media, 2015), loc. 249, Kindle.
14. Sam Allberry, *Why Bother with Church?: And Other Questions about Why You Need It and Why It Needs You*, Questions Christians Ask (Epsom, England: The Good Book Company, 2016), loc. 833, Kindle.
15. Annie Dillard, *Teaching a Stone to Talk: Expeditions and Encounters* (New York: Harper Perennial, 2013), 40.

HABIT #6: CARE FOR YOUR BODY

1. Usually attributed to Pierre Teilhard de Chardin, but probably derived from a quote by Wayne W. Dyer (see "You Are Not a Human Being Having a Spiritual Experience. You Are a Spiritual Being Having a Human Experience," Quote Investigator, June 20, 2019, https://quoteinvestigator.com/2019/06/20/spiritual/).
2. Millard J. Erickson, *Christian Theology*, 3rd ed. (Grand Rapids, MI: Baker Academic, 2013), 493, emphasis added.
3. R. Kent Hughes and Bryan Chapell, *1 & 2 Timothy and Titus: To Guard the Deposit*, Preaching the Word (Wheaton, IL: Crossway, 2000), 110.
4. Michael E. Wittmer, *Heaven Is a Place on Earth: Why Everything You Do Matters to God* (Grand Rapids, MI: Zondervan, 2004), loc. 880–87, Kindle.
5. Stacy Reaoch, "Exercise for More of God: Five Reasons to Train Your Body," Desiring God, May 16, 2019, https://www.desiringgod.org/articles/exercise-for-more-of-god.
6. Robert J. Karris, *Eating Your Way through Luke's Gospel* (Collegeville, MN: Liturgical Press, 2006), 14.
7. Robert Farrar Capon, *Supper of the Lamb: A Culinary Reflection* (New York: Farrar, Straus and Giroux, 1969), 17, Kindle.
8. Ibid., 40.
9. Asheritah Ciuciu, *Full: Food, Jesus, and the Battle for Satisfaction* (Chicago: Moody Publishers, 2017), 28.
10. Michael Pollan, *Food Rules: An Eater's Manual* (New York: Penguin Publishing Group, 2009), loc. 158, Kindle.
11. Ciuciu, *Full*, 18.
12. Michelle Segar, *No Sweat: How the Simple Science of Motivation Can Bring You a Lifetime of Fitness* (New York: AMACOM, 2015), 10, Kindle.
13. "Every Body Walk Documentary," YouTube, posted April 22, 2016, https://www.youtube.com/watch?v=6-NpTd3J7tg.
14. Erickson, *Christian Theology*, 493.

15. David Mathis, "A Little Theology of Exercise," Inspire 2020 Conference, Des Moines, March 22, 2020, Desiring God, https://www.desiringgod.org/messages/a-little-theology-of-exercise.
16. Segar, *No Sweat*, 14.

HABIT #7: SIMPLIFY AND PRIORITIZE

1. D. A. Carson, "Spiritual Disciplines," *Themelios* 36, no. 3 (2011): 378–79, https://www.thegospelcoalition.org/themelios/article/spiritual-disciplines/.
2. Eric Nels Ortlund (@EricNelsOrtlund), Twitter, March 10, 2021, https://twitter.com/EricNelsOrtlund/status/1369556675452166144.
3. Brett McCracken, *The Wisdom Pyramid: Feeding Your Soul in a Post-Truth World* (Wheaton, IL: Crossway, 2021), 33, Kindle.
4. Quoted in Robert Southey, *The Life of Wesley; and the Rise and Progress of Methodism*, vol. 1 (London: Longman, Hurst, Rees, Orme, and Brown, 1820), 33.
5. Timothy Keller, *Counterfeit Gods: The Empty Promises of Money, Sex, and Power, and the Only Hope That Matters* (New York: Riverhead Books, 2011), xvi.
6. Donald Guthrie, *Hebrews: An Introduction and Commentary*, vol. 15, Tyndale New Testament Commentaries (Downers Grove, IL: InterVarsity Press, 1983), 250.
7. Phil Knight, *Shoe Dog: A Memoir by the Creator of Nike* (New York: Scribner, 2016), loc. 610, Kindle.
8. Bob Goff, *Dream Big: Know What You Want, Why You Want It, and What You're Going to Do About It* (Nashville: Nelson Books, 2020), 144, Kindle.
9. Ibid., 145.
10. Dane Ortlund (@daneortlund), Twitter, August 7, 2020, https://twitter.com/daneortlund/status/1291693132254515200.

HABIT #8: GO THE DISTANCE

1. Ken Shigematsu, *God in My Everything: How an Ancient Rhythm Helps Busy People Enjoy God* (Grand Rapids, MI: Zondervan), 18, Kindle.
2. Stephen A. Macchia, *Crafting a Rule of Life: An Invitation to the Well-Ordered Way* (Downers Grove, IL: InterVarsity Press, 2012), loc. 114, Kindle.
3. Chip Heath and Dan Heath, *Switch: How to Change Things When Change Is Hard* (Toronto: Random House Canada, 2010), loc. 633, Kindle.
4. Ibid., loc. 533.

5. Robert E. Quinn and Garrett T. Quinn, *Letters to Garrett: Stories of Change, Power, and Possibility* (San Francisco: Jossey-Bass, 2002), 11–19.

6. Darryl Dash, "How a Rule of Life Helps Christians Live Well," *Faith Today*, April 23, 2017, https://www.faithtoday.ca/Magazines/2017-Mar-Apr/How-a-rule-of-life-helps-Christians-live-well.

7. Shigematsu, *God in My Everything*, 34.

8. Andrew M. Davis, *An Infinite Journey: Growing toward Christlikeness* (Greenville, SC: Ambassador International, 2014), loc. 138, Kindle.

9. Matthew B. Redmond, *The God Of The Mundane: Reflections on Ordinary Life for Ordinary People* (Murfreesboro, TN: Kalos Press, 2012), loc. 1093, Kindle.

10. Donald S. Whitney, *Spiritual Disciplines for the Christian Life* (Colorado Springs: NavPress, 2014), 289, Kindle.

11. Michael A. Eaton, *Ecclesiastes: An Introduction and Commentary*, Tyndale Old Testament Commentaries (Downers Grove, IL: InterVarsity, 1983), 48.

APPENDIX: SAMPLE PRACTICES

1. Douglas Kaine McKelvey and Ned Bustard, *Every Moment Holy*, vol. 1 (Nashville: Rabbit Room Press, 2020).

2. See Michael Hyatt, "How to Better Control Your Time by Designing Your Ideal Week," Michael Hyatt & Company, last updated April 6, 2011, https://michaelhyatt.com/ideal-week/.

ARE YOU DISSATISFIED WITH YOUR SPIRITUAL LIFE?

"God wants us to grow. But without a plan, growth will remain an aspiration instead of a reality. If you're interested in growing and helping others grow, then you'll appreciate this book."
ED STETZER EXECUTIVE DIRECTOR, BILLY GRAHAM CENTER AT WHEATON COLLEGE

APPLYING
THE GOSPEL
TO ALL OF YOUR LIFE

HOW TO GROW

DARRYL DASH

FOREWORD BY JARED C. WILSON

MOODY Publishers®

From the Word to Life®

How to Grow is for people who want to grow spiritually and help others grow as well. Darryl Dash demonstrates how the gospel continues to fuel transformation in the life of every believer long after conversion. Then he walks you through a practical, habit-based approach to spiritual growth.

978-0-8024-1819-7 | also available as an eBook